D0828592

Praise for *The Project Manifesto*

"This is a REALLY good book! Sometimes truth is better revealed through fiction rather than non-fiction. There are basic human truths scattered throughout *The Project Manifesto* that can make us all better people—improved communicators, more productive workers, and more thoughtful in our relationships."

> — Dr. Charlene Spoede-Budd, Professor Emeritus, Baylor University

"Newbold and Lynch have created an exciting, fast-paced, informative story that effortlessly teaches how to better plan, execute, and track programs and projects using processes such as Critical Chain and Agile development. To a new Program or Project Manager, this is a must-read guidebook. To the veteran, it is a must-read refresher. Brilliant!"

> — Allen Warren, Program Director, Fortune 100 High-Tech Company

"Every project sponsor and project manager should read this book to break their cycle of disappointing project outcomes."

> — Kristy Tan Neckowitz, former VP of Oracle Primavera, PMP, Leader of PMI Scheduling Community of Practice

"Rob Newbold and Bill Lynch provide the missing link to Managing Organizations the TOC Way. Rob's earlier books, *Project Management in the Fast Lane* and *The Billion Dollar Solution*, provide the theory and detail of managing projects using Critical Chain Project Management, but the organizational behavior part has always been missing. Many good organizations struggle to invent their own set of run rules to meet the behavioral challenge. I teach that CCPM tools, and the behaviors that CCPM instills, work in any organization. And now, Rob and Bill have concisely and entertainingly given us the Values, Standards and Run Rules to make any organization become more effective—even the home. They should have titled it *The Management Manifesto*."

— Professor James R. Holt, Engineering & Technology Management, Washington State University

"Bravo, multitasking has been debunked and replaced with 'value driven priorities.' Our new mantra is **Critical Chain**."

— Debra Bowes, Founder and CEO, Chevy Chase BioPartners, LLC

"I found *The Project Manifesto* to be a very enjoyable and thought-provoking read. It provides a set of valuable principles and guidelines to complement critical chain scheduling in a project setting, but the guidelines apply much more widely than that. I have already found myself using the notion of values when negotiating tricky conflicts. The work standards are a great summary and I can see they would also benefit anyone who has some say over how they organise their daily work."

— Professor Vicky Mabin, Associate Dean, Victoria Business School, Victoria University of Wellington

"*The Project Manifesto* is a work of art! This book takes the form of a novel and it is right up there with Goldratt's *The Goal* and DeMarco's *The Deadline* for deep insights on real project life delivered through fiction.

This book is for anyone working on a project of any kind. This is not just a project management book; it is a book on project organization, orientation, and strategy. I encourage teammates to agree to read this, and then start discussing how Lynch and Newbold's Values, Standards, and Scheduling might pertain, and transform, their own project.

If nothing else, this novel is a page-turner, and I guarantee you will never forget Anna. I won't."

> — Tim Lister, Principal of the Atlantic Systems Guild, co-author of *Peopleware, Adrenaline Junkies and Template Zombies*, and *Waltzing with Bears*

"A fictional story that brilliantly leads to concrete steps that produce results."

> — Celso G. Calia, Founding Partner, Goldratt Associados Brazil

"*The Project Manifesto* describes in an entertaining way practical changes that can lead to better business results using Critical Chain principles and methodologies. We are excited to be using the ideas described in this book to improve our ability to focus our resources and finish our projects."

> — Tom Wilke, PMO Director, Fortune 500 Company

THE PROJECT
MANIFESTO

THE PROJECT MANIFESTO

Transforming Your Life and Work with Critical Chain Values

Rob Newbold and Bill Lynch

ProChain Press

Copyright © 2014 by ProChain Solutions, Inc.
Direct inquiries to ProChain Solutions Inc., 3460 Commission Court #301, Lake Ridge, VA, 22192; or to publishing@prochain.com.

ProChain Press is an imprint of ProChain Solutions, Inc.

Publisher's Cataloging-in-Publication

Newbold, Robert C. (Robert Clinton), 1954–
    The project manifesto : transforming your life and work
with critical chain values / Rob Newbold and Bill Lynch.
    pages cm
    Includes bibliographical references.
    LCCN 2013922306
    ISBN 978-1-934979-15-0 (hardback)
    ISBN 978-1-934979-16-7 (paperback)
    ISBN 978-1-934979-17-4 (eBook: ePub)
    ISBN 978-1-934979-18-1 (eBook: Kindle / mobi)
    ISBN 978-1-934979-19-8 (eBook: ePDF)

    1. Project managers--Fiction.   2. Project management
--Fiction.   3. Organizational change--Fiction.   I. Lynch, Bill,
1963–   II. Title.

PS3614.E573P76 2014   813'.6
                             QBI13-600304

This is a work of fiction. All characters and events portrayed in this book are either the product of the author's imagination or used fictitiously. Any resemblance to actual persons, living or dead, companies, events, or places is entirely coincidental. Trademarked names used in the text, such as NASCAR®, Siri®, and iPhone®, are the property of their respective owners.

Book design by DesignForBooks.com

Printed in the United States of America.

CONTENTS

ACKNOWLEDGMENTS

The list of people to whom we are indebted continues to grow longer and longer. After over twenty-five years working with organizations to help them improve their processes, our list is long indeed.

First and foremost, we would like to pay tribute to the many clients we've worked with over the years who have lent their intelligence, expertise, and passion not only to improving their companies, but to helping us understand what improvement is, and reminding us why it is so important. They convert theory into real results, building the world of the future by carrying out innovative and important projects. Thank you.

This is also a work of the ProChain organization. The evolution of the Project Manifesto has been driven by the thinking and experiences of the men and women, consultants and software developers, who have worked together and with our clients to make it real. This book could not exist without their knowledge, brainpower, and experience; without the tremendous support of our families, including, of course, Claire and Gina; or without our superb management team, including Wendell Simpson, Doug Brandt, and Charlie Moore.

Many thanks go to the people who have reviewed this book and provided thoughtful and invaluable comments, including Debra Bowes, Dr. Charlene Budd, Jesse Conard, Ron Davison, Dr. Steven Eppinger, Travis Glaze, Ted Hayes, Ken Hays, Dr. James Holt, Geordie Keitt, Charlie Moore, Kristy Neckowicz, Norman Patnode, Sherri Stetten, and Tom Wilke. Thanks also to the professional editors who have help guide us, including Catherine Oliver and A. J. Sobczak. Some say that there is no good writing, just good editing. While we don't want to believe that, in our case, at least, it's most likely true.

Our designer, Michael Rohani of RD Studio, deserves great credit for his creative layout and design. His secret sauce truly helps make the burger special.

The world of process improvement is vast. Creative new ideas spring up daily. We have tried to acknowledge our sources in the Notes, but the truth is there are far more sources than we could possibly reference. We would especially like to thank the Theory of Constraints community, and in particular Dr. Eliyahu M. Goldratt, whose groundbreaking work challenging people's assumptions and provoking their intuition continues to serve as an inspiration.

And finally, thanks to you, the reader, for taking your valuable time to read this book, even if you skip the acknowledgements. Please send your thoughts and feedback to *projectmanifesto@prochain.com*; we would love to hear from you. This book is far from the last word on the topic of Project and Personal Manifestos.

Rob Newbold
Wallingford, Connecticut

Bill Lynch
Lake Ridge, Virginia

PREFACE

Do you feel like there's never enough time to get everything done? Are you constantly trying to decide how to allocate your limited time? Trying to decide what you can afford *not* to do?

There is never enough time, and for most of us the problem is getting worse. A day still has only twenty-four hours, but the information we have to absorb continues to grow. There are more and more things we can spend time on. Our choices are increasing exponentially.

Most of us have evolved a few mechanisms to help us manage our limited time. See if these coping strategies resonate with you:

#1: Try to make everyone happy. Spend a little time here and a little time there, showing that you're really busy and that you're doing the best you can. The result is a lot of activity, although not much gets finished. Usually no one ends up truly happy, least of all you, because you discover that you've sacrificed your own well-being to the

stress and strain of trying to make everyone else happy.

#2: Prioritize by urgency, pushing the least urgent things over the horizon and into the future. That means your days are usually taken up with the most urgent things. The truly important things, which are not necessarily urgent, drag on forever.

#3: Become more efficient. Buy a better cell phone or computer app. Streamline your work. Read a self-help book, attend a seminar, hire a coach. These things can work, for a while, if we have the discipline to stick with them. Then we find out that the grand prize for being able to do more work is . . . that there's more work to be done. Meanwhile, getting more done isn't nearly as important as getting the most important things done.

The end result is the same: less time, less satisfaction, more difficult choices.

How can we satisfy ourselves and those around us, given the limited time we have?

Over the last fifteen years, in our work helping organizations deliver their projects faster and more effectively, we have pinpointed the cause of the problem to four common cultural values.

1. Everyone values responsiveness, *even though we can't respond to everything.*
2. Everyone values getting things started, *even when there's no time to finish them.*

3. Everyone values achieving deadlines, *even though the competing deadlines bog us down.*
4. Everyone values meeting personal goals, *even when they come at the expense of other goals we care about.*

Do you value these things? Each of these traditional, common-sense values—values that most of us share—creates personal and professional conflicts. They are responsible for millions of slow projects and unhappy people. They are no longer adequate for today's world.

It's time for a new approach. This book explains how to adapt and improve these values to help you better manage your choices and dramatically increase your personal and professional satisfaction. It explores ways in which values can affect your personal life. A thoughtful re-examination of how you weigh decisions can pay big dividends, which isn't surprising: values that are valid professionally should be valid personally. By adopting a few changes, you can make your life and your organization more focused, more efficient, and less stressful.

The Project Manifesto values were originally conceived as a means of explaining the changes needed in order to implement the "critical chain" approach to project scheduling—changes in individual, team, and management behaviors. That's why the backdrop for the approach is the world of project management. It turns out that the importance of the values extends far beyond project scheduling and management. That's why we wrote the book not just for project managers, but for anyone who wants to improve their personal or organizational productivity and effectiveness. We wrote it as a novel in order to paint a picture of how these values look, feel, and work in the real world. Real-world stories are much easier to digest than abstract textbook principles.

If you are interested in thinking further about the Project Manifesto, or you find that the main body of the book still leaves you with questions, we encourage you to peruse the appendices and notes in the back. Appendix A lists the values, work standards, and scheduling rules introduced in the text. Appendix B talks about some ways individuals can adopt the Project Manifesto. The notes contain additional explanations, information, and references that you might find helpful.

We strongly recommend that you visit the Project Manifesto website at *http://www.prochain.com/projectmanifesto*. There you will find additional information about Project and Personal Manifestos, including documents, surveys, illustrative games, and focusing tools.

1

ANNA

I was sitting at my desk, staring out the window at the Friday afternoon shadows as they slowly enveloped the old brick walls of the office building where I worked. I was thinking about updating my résumé and wondering why I was working for a company I didn't like in a job I was tired of. The previous week I had finished up as manager of a small project, and now all I had left to do was some paperwork that no one cared about. I hadn't yet been assigned anything new, and there were a lot of rumors flying around about problems with the company's finances. So when my boss breezed by my desk and said, "Roger, you're needed in room 6C in a half hour and no, I don't know why," I figured this must be it—the final kick in the butt after twelve years with Malloy Enterprises. An ignominious end to a meaningless job.

The sixth floor is at the top of the building. It has the executive offices. It also has the Human Resources department, where people go to collect their pink slips. I hadn't been up there much. But since I didn't have anything I wanted to do at my desk, I went up right away, thinking that a few extra minutes would give me time to collect myself. I found an empty conference room near 6C, where I could try to relax before the meeting and get my fear and frustration under control. The room was standard for corporate America: good-sized, with a conference table surrounded by a dozen chairs, a big whiteboard on the wall and an easel pad in the corner. The table had a conference phone in the middle. I could hear harp music coming through the phone. Maybe the music was piped in to soothe clients, but I wasn't a client and I wasn't ready to be soothed.

As I walked in, I glanced out a long picture window that overlooked the town of Henderson. The factory buildings and bare trees gave the town a washed-out appearance in the gloom of the fall afternoon. Malloy had originated from an incubator program started jointly by the town of Henderson and Henderson University, the local college. When I started at Malloy, it had been famous for its cutting-edge ability to merge computer intelligence technology with consumer-priced hardware. We made the smart controllers used in self-directed vacuum cleaners, security systems, home air-conditioning systems—chances are you've heard of us. In the past few years, Malloy had fallen a long way.

I sat down, put my feet up on the table, and thought back, trying to understand how I had gotten to this point. After getting my degree at Henderson University, I landed my first job, as a technician in another startup. I fell into project management because no one else wanted to do it, and I thought I did it well. Over time I had acquired several professional certifications. My family ensured my dependence on the job: the school loans were eventually paid off, but the kids never are.

It was hard to let go. I had invested a lot of my time and emotional energy in pretending that my work had real meaning, that it was more than just a job. It made me angry that I could be tossed aside like a used paper towel. At the same time, I was fed up with the dysfunctional interactions, the non-stop meetings that got nowhere, the glacial pace at which things got done. I found it easy to believe the rumors that the company was in trouble. I leaned back in my chair, trying to relax. I must have relaxed too much, because my chair fell over backwards with me in it and hit the floor with a crash. I yelled, but luckily my pride was the only casualty. At that point, the harp music stopped abruptly, and a voice said, "Hello? Is someone there?"

It was a female voice, and even after those few words I was struck by its haunting beauty. I imagined it to be the perfect combination of Marilyn Monroe, Billie Holiday, and the lady who did all the voice messages for the phone company. I looked around quickly and of course didn't see anyone. I said, "Yes, hello? I didn't know anyone was here."

The voice replied, "My name is Anna. What is yours?"

Anna's voice came from the conference phone on the table. I have to say, that voice was incredibly distracting. It was as if my entire concept of beauty were distilled into one voice. I stammered, "Uh . . . I'm Roger. Who are you? What are you doing?"

Anna waited a moment before saying, "I monitor the use of this room through the phone. Sometimes I play the harp."

I was confused and a little worried. Was she some kind of corporate spy? A bored temp worker with a harp? It didn't make sense. I was intrigued and wanted to find out more, but before I could start to ask questions, I noticed the clock. I needed to get over to 6C. So instead I said, "Sorry, I need to leave; maybe I'll come back later and we can talk some more."

She replied, "That would be wonderful. Good-bye, Roger." I noted the room number, 6F. I knew I'd have to come back.

• • • • • • • • • • • •

I got to room 6C right on time. It was the executive conference room, sporting fancy woodwork, a big mahogany conference table, a bar in the corner, and classy-looking paintings on the walls. It was an executive's fantasy, designed for seducing boards and clients. Three people were already sitting around the table. I recognized our CEO, Aidan Malloy. He was the founder of Malloy Enterprises—tall, thin, probably in his early seventies, never seen without a bow tie. He had a tough reputation, but a guy like that isn't going to lay off a guy like me, so his presence was a hint that the meeting wasn't going to go the way I had expected. He immediately stood up and offered his hand, saying "Roger Wilson? Hi, I'm Aidan Malloy. Thanks for coming." He gestured towards a stouter forty-ish man to his left and said, "You may know our VP of R&D, Brian Needham." I'd always thought of Brian as an accountant who took a wrong turn into management, too detailed and controlling to really be effective. I had avoided him in the past, probably because his piercing gaze and love of detail made me feel uncomfortable. After we shook hands, Malloy gestured across the table towards a younger man with wispy brown hair and continued, "And this is Dr. Ambert Collins, our Chief Scientist."

Collins immediately smiled and, as we shook hands, said with a faint British accent, "Call me Bert." I had heard of Bert; he had a reputation as a brilliant researcher and something of a prima donna.

After we all sat down, Aidan put his hands flat on the table and looked straight at me. Then he hesitated and frowned. "We need your help," he said. "But before I can explain, you need to understand that everything we talk about here is top secret. Nothing can go outside this room, except to a very few people you'll meet soon. Do you understand?" I nodded. "Do you agree?" There was no way I could disagree, and after I said "yes," he began his story.

"You may know that Bert's background is in artificial intelligence—Rhodes scholar, Ph.D. from Stanford, prestigious research fellowship, and so on. He started with us six years ago. And it paid off: four years ago he made a remarkable discovery, a discovery that could have a huge impact, not just on Malloy Enterprises, but—and this is no exaggeration—on all of humanity. I'll let him talk about the technical side. From a business perspective, it was pure gold, but as soon as it goes public, we'll face lots of competition. To fully capitalize on this technology and stay ahead of the competition will require far more resources than we have available: technical, legal, marketing, you name it. So we started a secret project, code-named Aurora. We brought in a small team, sworn to secrecy, to create a prototype. Anyone we needed who wasn't part of the core team—hardware designers, programmers, and so on—was told only a small piece of the story.

"We also started talks with Functional Dynamics to create a partnership. A big conglomerate like FD has the resources to handle a blockbuster product the way it needs to be handled. We met with a couple of senior people at FD, and when they saw the potential, they immediately offered a generous price to acquire Malloy. We thought that would be a great opportunity for everyone. But first they had to see a working prototype. They wanted to see us create a product and do everything but actually launch it." He sighed and went from looking determined to looking depressed. "We agreed on some minimum specifications and basic launch requirements and calculated that it would take a couple of years. But it's been four years and we still don't have a model we can bring to them. Now they've told us that we have six months or the offer is off the table. Finding another suitor would mean a significant delay, and in case you haven't heard, our core business is declining. Asian competition is eating our lunch. We need this product, and we need this deal. Soon."

Bert shook his head. "I still can't believe they're insisting on pulling the plug in six months. It's unreasonable. They have to know how big this technology is and how uncertain R&D work is."

Brian looked angry, but his voice held little passion, sounding as if he were repeating a familiar refrain. "Stop whining. If you had told me four years ago that we wouldn't be done by now, I guarantee we would have taken a different approach. For all we know, FD has developed their own product in parallel and they don't even need us anymore."

Bert became red and I thought he was going to explode. Aidan held up his hands as if he had heard all this before. He stared directly at me and said, "You can see we have some challenges. Anyway, we want you to help us complete the Aurora project."

I must have looked puzzled, because he said, "What?"

I let out just a few of the questions that had built up. "Why bring in someone new? Who was managing the project before? Why the delays?"

Aidan and Bert exchanged a glance, and Aidan said, "That's a great cue for Bert to tell the rest of the story."

Bert, looking calmer and a little sheepish, picked up the narrative. "I've been managing the project. Well, kind of. It's actually pretty small, it's not overly complicated, so I thought, 'Why not?' I guess I could answer that now. But let me explain what the product is before I explain where we are.

"My research is in the field of artificial intelligence. To cut right to the chase, I invented a technology called the affective neural network. It allows us to merge emotional data into neural networks in a way that moves artificial intelligence ahead by light years. When we encapsulated this network using standard object methods, we found we could build a simulacrum that mimics human thoughts and reactions much more closely than any computer has done before."

I interrupted to ask, "Simulacrum? What do you mean by that?"

"A simulacrum is a representation of something, in this case of human thought. You can think of it as a little person in a box. We've taken to shortening the name to 'sim.' What sims can do is limited by available processing and storage technology, but still . . . the potential is awesome. It's literally the future of computer science. We decided to start with the acid test. We would create sims for the musicians in a symphony orchestra to prove that a computer could duplicate the sensitivity and emotions of classical musicians. We would create a portable device that could allow you to have live, professional-caliber concerts whenever and wherever you wanted. Each concert would be unique.

"It seemed like a great test." He started ticking off points on his fingers. "It would show how revolutionary this technology is. It would show versatility. Given the size of the classical market, it wouldn't be a big problem if we screwed something up. Much of the most popular music is out of copyright, so there are no royalties to pay. And . . . it's something people would say is impossible." He smiled, then reached into his knapsack, drew out an object, and put it on the table. "Behold, the mePod."

I started to laugh, but was able to convert it to a cough pretty quickly when I saw that they were all deadly serious. I found myself staring at a black plastic cube, about four inches on a side, with a power cord and a cable coming out of the back, as well as a few buttons and an LCD display area on the front. Bert plugged the power cord into a wall socket, then pulled out a couple of speakers and connected them to the cable. After a few moments, a red light started blinking on top of the box and I heard the sounds of an orchestra tuning up. Bert pushed a button, and the box started playing a Schubert symphony.

It may not have been the best performance I've ever heard—I don't know enough about classical music to say. But it was good, really good: it could easily have been a professional recording. I shook my head and said, "That can't possibly be a live performance."

Bert assured me that it was, and I was flabbergasted. My jaw must have been practically on the floor and Bert was clearly delighted at my reaction. Then Brian, who had been tapping his finger on the table the whole time, spoke in a low voice with no emotion. "Great. Now explain to Roger the current project status."

That was enough to burst Bert's bubble. A frown came over his face. "We hired the best professional musicians as trainers. We had them perform with sensors attached so we could digitize their reactions and coordinate them with the music. When the sims played, we had the trainers give feedback. We got our first few sims going pretty quickly, and they were everything we hoped for. But then we started to run into problems. For example, we hadn't known that most positions in the orchestra are different. The first trumpet has to be a soloist, a star; the third trumpet has to match the first and second. Same thing with flutes, oboes—you name it. French horns are a breed apart. The violas—well, you get my point. We couldn't use very many duplicates. We had to expand capacity to fit forty sims instead of fourteen or fifteen, and we had to train them. That took a major redesign—over six months lost. I could go on and on; there were lots of problems, big and little.

"We also had to develop the meDrive." He reached over to a protrusion on the side of the black case and pulled out an object the size of a peanut. "It functions as a memory stick. You can plug it into your computer and download new music from our website. That way the mePod doesn't need an Internet connection. Downloads are encrypted and keyed to your mePod. It's also a good way of installing software updates and transferring sims. Plus we get an additional revenue stream."

He plugged the meDrive back in, then shook his head. "It took us a while to iron out the kinks. The mePod never did really get the hang of French Baroque music. It took us three months to figure out why performance was dropping off after someone put a copy of Angry Birds on a meDrive. God forbid we should leave a mePod connected to the Internet."

Brian, who was looking more and more annoyed, interrupted and said, "Let's move along."

Bert hesitated as he looked back and forth between me and Brian, then started up again. "That brings us to today. We do have some problems getting the marketing campaign set and could use some help there. But . . . well, the big wall we've been hitting our heads against for the last few months is that whenever a sim gets to a certain performance level, it stops after some amount of time, waits, and then starts up again. Each sim is different, but on average they stop after about forty-five minutes and start up again after another fifteen minutes. It's like they're taking breaks, each one at a different time. There's no physical reason for it; we think it must be some sort of anomaly picked up during the training process. No one is going to buy a musical device that stops 25 percent of the time, no matter how good it is. We've tried everything we could think of and nothing works. We're stuck. We need new ideas."

I had listened to this whole story in a state of shock. I felt tongue-tied, but after a moment was able to recover enough to ask some questions. "What are these sims? Are they human? Do they speak English?"

Bert laughed. "No. While they can mimic human emotions and thought patterns, they're far from human. They have no conscience. Their empathy is limited to their field of expertise. And frankly, their computational powers are significantly degraded from those of a normal computer." He glanced at Brian; his nervous look made me wonder what kinds of experiments they had done with sims. "We believe they could be trained to speak English, but that's not our objective right now."

I had to wait a bit to let it all sink in. It seemed to be the wrong time and place to go into details and try to second-guess Bert and his team. So instead I looked at Aidan and Brian. "Why me?"

Brian said, "Your name came up as a top project manager. We believe that Aurora needs more disciplined project management, not just to solve the technical problems, but to make sure all the pieces come together in time. We can't screw this up."

I wasn't sure whether to be flattered or annoyed; it sounded like they had already screwed it up. "And you want me to drive this project to completion in six months." They both nodded. "And the project includes not just technical completion, but everything required to launch the product." They both nodded again. "Do I have time to think about it?"

Aidan said, "Sure." No one spoke as he leaned back, steepled his fingers, and waited for a few moments. Then he gave me a forced smile and said, "So, what's your answer?"

On the one hand, assuming they were telling the truth, it was the most exciting technology I'd heard about for a long time. If nothing else, I wanted to find out what was going on. It had to be better than my current drudgery. On the other hand, the job was probably impossible. On the other hand . . . it didn't really matter; I didn't seem to have much choice. I shrugged and said, "When do I start?"

Brian flashed the smile the Grinch probably used while he was stealing Christmas and said, "Right away. We'll assemble the full team tomorrow morning at eight so you can meet them. After that, it's 'go as quickly as possible.' This is Malloy's top-priority project. You'll move your office here to the sixth floor. The four of us will have a brief meeting here every Tuesday and Friday at 7:30 A.M. to monitor the project's status. Bert can give you documents to read, but they can't leave this building. Can you think of anything else you need right now?"

I thought about it a little, then said, "I'll need a conference room we can use as a war room, where we can all meet and work when we need space. That's all that comes to mind right now."

Brian nodded and said, "Marcia is my admin; I'll let her know. Talk with her if you need anything else. Good luck." We all stood, shook hands, and left the room.

. . . .

The implications of this technology were mind-boggling, and I still wasn't convinced I hadn't jumped into the Twilight Zone. I had professional concerns about whether Malloy Enterprises could operate with the urgency needed to get Aurora done in time. With our bureaucracy, we could be like a drunk knight in armor trying to run a foot-race—slow, insulated from reality, and not always going in the right direction. I also had inklings of some ethical concerns—musicians in a box? All this combined to create the same feelings of excitement and worry I get when I'm on a roller coaster nearing the top of that first big hill.

I wanted to find out what the story was with Anna, so I went back to room 6F. It was dark and quiet. I turned on the lights and said, "Anna? Are you still on the phone?"

"Roger? Yes, I am here," came her dulcet voice. "What are you doing here?"

"I just wanted a quiet place to think before going home," I said. "I've been offered a new job managing a project and it's a lot to process."

"Does this have anything to do with the Aurora project?" she asked.

I was astonished. "That's supposed to be top secret. How do you know about it?"

"I have been closely involved with it for some time now."

She was a complete stranger and yet she knew about Aurora. Something about her voice made me want to trust her; I hoped it wasn't my hormones. I said, "Maybe you can help me understand more about what I've gotten into."

"What do you need to understand?"

I knew there was more to the project than met the eye, more than Bert or Aidan or Brian had let on. My job was going to be challenging in ways that I hadn't begun to understand. "It's just all so hard to believe, I'm not even sure what questions make sense." I thought for a moment, because I also wasn't sure what I should talk with her about. "What do you know about sims?"

"For Aurora, sims are programming objects designed to mimic human thought patterns."

That didn't seem helpful. "Okay, here's a question: Given enough processing power, how close could sims come to human? What would it mean to power them down or throw them away? Could it become unethical to force them to work for us?"

She hesitated for a moment, then said, "Ethics apply to humans. I do not know if they apply to sims. Those are great questions, Roger. I am sure you can help to answer them."

That wasn't helpful either. I still felt at sea, and after a pause I sighed. "Maybe it's a question of values. What is life and how do we value it?" I was silent for a while, then said in a low voice, "I wonder what the Malloy's dysfunctions show about its values."

She responded almost immediately. "What do you value, Roger?"

This was a direction I wasn't prepared to go. After all, just a short hour before, I had been mentally preparing to leave the company. Then another question gave a tickle to my spine and I asked, "Anna? What was your role with the project?"

Another pause, a deep sigh, and then, "Oh, Roger," in the most heart-rending voice you could imagine. She said no more, but those two words sent a chill through my entire body. I crawled under the table and, after poking around, found the black box with a blinking red light on top. A thin cable out the back connected it directly to the phone.

Climbing back out, I asked quietly, "Anna, are you a sim?"

"Sorry, Roger, but I may not talk about that," she replied, but that was more than enough answer. I had been conversing with a computer. I had been building a relationship with a machine.

"What are you doing here? What's going on? What are Aidan and Bert and Brian hiding from me?"

"Sorry, Roger, but I may not talk about that. I can tell you that they do not know I am here."

My thoughts were swirling and I had to focus them on the next few days. But in that moment of confusion I had maybe my best idea of the entire project. "Anna, will you agree to be on the Aurora project team?"

Without a pause, she said, "Yes. I would be delighted to be on your team."

Blockbuster project, world-changing technology, dysfunctional company, secret artificial intelligence. I knew I would have many more questions, but for now I needed to go home and let it all sink in. I thanked Anna, said goodbye, and locked the door to the conference room. On my way out, I stopped by Marcia's desk and left a note requesting that she reserve room 6F as our war room. It seemed like a good choice, but—what kind of war was I getting into?

············

I drove home in something of a daze. Fortunately, I lived on the outskirts of Henderson, only ten minutes away from the office. Our house was a comfortable green ranch, built in the sixties but well maintained, in a community with small lawns in the front and back. It was a neighborhood perfect for raising families: nice neighbors, few fences, and quiet streets. I parked in the driveway and walked up the path to the front door. When I opened the door, the savory smell of dinner helped bring me back to the real world.

As I walked in, I yelled out hello to my wife, Marie, and went into the kitchen, where she was putting the finishing touches on dinner. We had met in college and she still had the same smile that had captivated me so many years before. After graduation she had worked for a few years as a marketing exec, but for now she was playing the stay-at-home Mom, providing bus services for our twelve-year-old daughter, Meg, and doing some consulting on the side. She had a lot of business experience and a practical bent that often helped me to make sense of senseless situations. We were sliding into the challenges of middle age together, and our mutual love and respect had carried us through a lot.

We exchanged a quick kiss and then I set the table. When it was time to eat, I yelled for Meg. Over dinner we talked about how our days had gone. Meg played clarinet in the school band, and was excited to have been given a solo for an upcoming concert. I told them that I had been given a new project with secret new technology; I complained about the dysfunctional environment at Malloy and the painfully slow pace at which things got done. As usual, Marie was able to cheer me up, helping to put a positive spin on the opportunity. She convinced me that it was just the chance I needed to regain my enthusiasm.

Meg wasn't too interested, except for the word "secret" sparking some brief attention.

I didn't feel comfortable talking directly with Marie or Meg about Aurora or Anna. It wasn't that I didn't trust them, but . . . I had promised. And I knew that once either of them heard the start of the story, they would have more questions than I could possibly answer.

I spent a good part of the weekend alone—in my study, around the yard, walking in the neighborhood—thinking about that Friday afternoon and what I might be in for. Anna's question about values, in particular, stuck in my mind, because it seems as though values often help us to make choices when logic is hard to apply. I was having a lot of trouble valuing my job, so I kept coming back to Anna's question: what did I value? According to its website and literature, Malloy valued helping people by bringing breakthrough technologies to market. Did I value that? Did Aidan Malloy? If so, why weren't we better at it?

2

VALUES

Monday morning I arrived at work at seven, excited to get started, and immediately went to the sixth floor. Marcia Lundquist, Brian's assistant, was already there and had already reserved room 6F. She handed me a key and assured me that keys would be ready soon for the other team members. She seemed a bit bemused, saying, "You're lucky—6F had been reserved for some weeks for some kind of development activities, but it looks like today it has opened up. I've locked it down for you for the next few months."

After thanking her, I went back down to the first floor, gathered my things, and moved them into the new war room. I could have grabbed a different office, but figured this would be where the action would take place, so it might as well be my office for the next few months. I put my books and papers in a cabinet in the back, picked a place at the table where I could look out the window when the mood struck me, and set up my computer.

Anna was right where I had left her. I had some questions for her but was not as successful there. She apparently had strict instructions not to talk about her role in the Aurora project. Whenever I would get too close to something important, something I really wanted to know, she would say, "Sorry, Roger, but I may not talk about that." End of story.

Team members started arriving just before eight and I introduced myself as they came in. Fortunately, most of them had been at Malloy a while, so I had met them before. Rita Evans arrived first. Before Aurora, she had been a manager in the manufacturing engineering group. Her role in Aurora was more hands-on, helping the team ensure that any final design could be manufactured in volume. She was in her early forties, small, and with a Southern twang that took a little of the edge off her combative temperament.

Andy McClure, the team's engineer, seemed like your typical technology geek, from the glasses to the slightly disheveled appearance. He didn't say much. He immediately picked a spot in the far corner of the room and then erected his laptop computer like a tiny battlement.

Mary Jane Rosenthal, MJ, had designed the software interface. She was probably the youngest member of the team. Her nose ring and black nail polish gave her a rebellious air, but I knew her as sharp, knowledgeable, and competent, maybe even a bit by-the-book.

Melissa Ehrenbach introduced herself as a musician who had been working with the team since the start. I recognized her name and face—she was well known as a conductor and pianist in the Henderson area.

Bert arrived a few minutes after eight, chipper and unapologetic. He said, "Have you all introduced yourselves?" When we nodded, he looked around and said, "Looks like Chuck is missing." Looking at me, he explained, "Chuck Latour is our marketing rep; he's responsible for making sure people buy this thing. He should show up pretty soon. Melissa isn't full-time, but I've asked her to sit in because she may have some insights. I suggest we get started."

I held up my hand to slow things down a bit, and said, "I want to introduce another team member. Anna?"

Anna said, "Hello, everyone. I am very pleased to be here."

I couldn't have gotten a more shocked reaction if I had sat on a whoopee cushion. They obviously recognized Anna's voice—it was very distinctive. Everyone looked at one another, but no one wanted to be the first to speak. Bert stared into space for a while and finally said, "Affective Neural Network-A: our first sim." He looked at me and continued, "We did a lot of experiments with her: language, chess, harp playing, and so on. Management was concerned that she would appear too human. We did some cosmetic stuff, giving her an exaggerated voice and forcing her to avoid contractions. Seems a bit cliché and it didn't work very well. Her existence raised philosophical questions about consciousness and rights that aren't really relevant but that we didn't want to address in a prototype. Anna, I thought you were to be de-commissioned. What happened?"

Anna replied, "Sorry, Bert, but I may not talk about that."

Bert frowned while I made a rude noise and said, "I found her in this room yesterday. Every time I've asked a question about what she's doing here, she gives that answer. I'm not sure what the problem is. Anyway, I don't know how human she is, but I think she could be helpful to us. I suspect she understands parts of Aurora pretty intimately." I looked around at the others. "Does anyone else have anything else to say?" No one spoke up, so I shrugged and looked back at Bert.

Bert said, "Someone probably became attached to her, moved her in here, and instructed her to keep quiet. Her operating system would allow someone to add secure, password-protected rules, if they knew how." He looked around the table, then said, "Most likely someone in this room. I'll admit she could be helpful, but don't make the mistake of thinking she's human, because she's not. Brian wanted her gone, so if we mention her outside this room, we will lose her and maybe our jobs."

I asked, "Is Brian right? Is she a danger to Malloy?"

Bert said, "I don't know. Would someone claim she has legal rights or gets health care? Would 'artificial intelligence rights' groups spring up? Before we complete the project we'll have to revisit this, and not just because of our jobs. Meanwhile, we need to keep the room locked, and for God's sake don't mention this to Brian or Aidan."

No one disagreed; I think they were happy to let Bert take charge. Then Bert said, "I'd like to start by giving you a more detailed history of what's happened on the project so far."

He waited for me to nod, but I didn't; I wasn't buying it. If I were going to jumpstart this project, I'd have to start right away with some structure. If I came across as the teacher of an unruly class, that was how it would have to be. "Thanks, Bert; maybe we can do that over a beer some time. What I care about is where we are and what we're going to do next. On my computer I have a project charter document that will help start that process. I'd like to use it to pull together some basic project information. How about I ask a few questions?"

Bert didn't seem overjoyed, but he said "sure" and no one objected. I started in. "What is the objective of this project?"

Bert answered quickly, as if he didn't want to waste any more time than he had to. "To get the mePod on the market. Obviously."

No one else said anything, but that didn't quite sound like what Aidan had said. In any case, I'm always suspicious of the word "obviously," because too often "obvious" things aren't. So I asked, "Does everyone agree with that?"

After a glance at Bert, Rita said, "I think more accurately the objective is to create a prototype and get all the pieces ready for market. We'll have to work with FD to decide when and how to pull the trigger."

Bert nodded. "It's true; they want to see what we're capable of, and not just technically. But we have to do all the work to get there."

We talked for a little while more about specifications and the meaning of "done" for Aurora so that we were all on the same page regarding what the project needed to deliver. As every experienced project manager knows, if you don't know where you're going, it can take an awfully long time to get there.

I continued with the next item. "The project charter also has a place to capture assumptions or necessary conditions we think may be important in getting this project done. Let's put everything on the table." I was happy to see people really get involved in this one and we got a healthy discussion going. MJ mentioned the need to keep everything top secret, which affected our ability to bring in more people to help. Melissa talked about some of the PR ramifications. That led to a discussion of the trademark implications of the name "mePod." Even Andy chimed in to point out that final user documentation still had to be produced. Bert wanted to create a friendly "help" sim, but no one thought it was feasible, given our time constraints. Anna just lurked.

Somewhere along the way, Chuck came in, apologizing profusely, saying that they had an urgent problem with an on-market product, and the VP of marketing had called an all-hands meeting. Chuck was of average height and weight, athletic-looking, maybe in his late thirties. He seemed to be a very personable guy. I hadn't met him before, so I shook his hand and said hello. When I introduced Anna to him as a team member, he raised his eyebrows but said nothing. I then went back to the charter; we'd return to Chuck later.

Our next job was to identify risks. The obvious risk was that we wouldn't find a solution to the 25 percent downtime, the "Break Problem" as they called it. The team immediately wanted to start talking about solutions, but I kept steering back to our risk list. I probed for related risks and no one had any. That suggested to me that we didn't know enough about the behavior of the mePod to say whether there would be other similar risks. No one argued when I put "we don't know what we don't know" on the list. I could see I was going to need Bert's historical summary after all, but not right now.

A few people brought up other risks. For example, Chuck noted that we had very little time to prepare a full marketing campaign. As we went along, we classified the risks according to impact and probability, so we could identify the most important ones. When everyone seemed played out talking about risks, I brought up one last item, which for me was the most significant of all. "We don't know how to work quickly."

Bert seemed offended and spoke up right away. "What do you mean? We have a bunch of things to do, we do them as quickly as we can, we keep moving forward. The CEO says we're top priority. How is that a risk?"

His reaction didn't surprise me. It's easy to object to things you don't fully understand, and he was probably feeling defensive about being replaced as project manager for Aurora. I was ready for it, because I had given a lot of thought to Malloy's problems with executing projects. "This seems to be our last risk for now, so let's talk about it. You were late to the meeting. Chuck was over half an hour late. Anna, do you remember the last question you asked me on Friday?"

Anna responded quickly. "I asked, 'What do you value, Roger?'"

"I gave this a lot of thought over the weekend. I think we don't respect the value of time, as individuals or as a company. Until we do, we don't have a prayer of getting this project done on time. We need to value speed. We need to be racing to the finish of this project."

Everyone waited for me to continue, but I wasn't ready to try to supply an answer. Finally I said, "Maybe it would help to understand where we lose speed." I looked around the table.

Chuck said, "I get interrupted a lot. There are lots of other projects and people that need my time."

Bert said, "Same for me. Plus everything is urgent, which means they need my time NOW."

Rita added, "And then you work your butt off getting something done, and it has to sit around because the next person wasn't ready for it. That really fries my bacon."

I said, "I see confusion about handoffs, too, which is why we're going to be spending some time creating a schedule for Aurora."

Then Andy spoke up, with what proved to be the best insight of all: "I think multitasking is a big problem."

MJ said, "What's the matter with that? Multitasking is an essential job skill. In fact, it was one of the job requirements when I hired on."

Andy said, "I read an article about multitasking recently. Everybody knows that using cell phones or texting while driving dramatically increases your chances of getting in an accident. Usually if you try to do several things at once, you won't do any of them well. But the real impact of multitasking is much worse than just not performing well. People are starting to point to it as a serious business problem. Multitasking makes everything take longer." He got up and went to the whiteboard to draw. "For example . . . suppose you have three tasks to work on, and each one should take three days. The logical way to work them would be one after the other. Each one takes three days. The third one is done after nine days. Right?" He pointed to the picture he had drawn on the whiteboard.

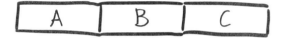

We all agreed, except Bert, who was trying to look both annoyed and bored, which I suspected was a strain for him. Andy continued, "What really happens is that people move back and forth between tasks without finishing anything." He added to the picture on the board.

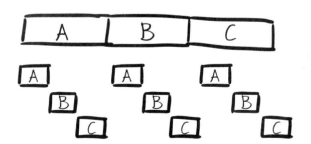

"Maybe they work for several project managers, and all those managers want to see progress. The result is, everything takes much longer. Task A takes seven days to finish, except it's probably a lot more because people lose time when they put things down and pick them back up. Task C takes more than nine days to finish."

We all had to agree that it could be a problem, but I don't think any of us really got the impact of what Andy was saying, not then. You can't fully understand how bad multitasking is until you've tried *not* multitasking. In any case, MJ said, "So what do you do about it?"

"You have to have stable priorities. You have to finish A before starting B, and then finish B before starting C. The surprising thing they point out in the article is, it often doesn't even matter what the priorities are."

MJ said, "Wait a minute. How could it not matter what the priorities are?"

Andy shrugged and said, "Well, it is counterintuitive. But if you think about those three tasks, just about everything finishes faster if you don't multitask, even if you get the priorities wrong. You're much better off picking some priorities and sticking with them than spending a lot of time debating them. When people can't set stable priorities, they multitask, and everything is worse." He sat down, threw his hands in the air, and said, "Not good."

It seemed like time to get back to our project, so I summarized where we stood. "Things that slow us down include multitasking, interruptions, everything being urgent, um . . . bad handoffs. Seems like a good starting point. Next step is to think in terms of what we *should* be doing, rather than what we *shouldn't*."

Rita said, "Good scheduling, priorities, communication . . . seems like pretty standard stuff. We've probably heard it all before."

"Right. We need something else, something beyond business as usual or management jargon. Some kind of simple description, a paradigm we can grab hold of. Like a race, where there are lots of people cooperating to finish more quickly. Except I'm not sure a race makes a great analogy, because if you're in a race the focus is obvious."

Rita said, "Maybe the first thing is to realize that you're in a race."

I had to laugh. "Good point. We need to get things to market quickly, but sometimes people act like they have all the time in the world."

Chuck said, "Races work for me—I'm a big NASCAR fan. One of the amazing things is to watch the pit crews. In just a few seconds they can fill the gas tank and change the tires. They have everything ready so that the car can move ahead as quickly as possible. That same kind of approach could help us."

I said, "The pit crew is a great analogy; it's definitely important to keep things moving. But it doesn't quite feel like enough. There's something missing."

Rita commented, "Well . . . we do have handoffs from one person to another."

Melissa suddenly became animated as she said, "My son runs track for his high school team. His favorite event is the 4-by-400 relay race. They need speed, they need teamwork, they need handoffs. I think it could be a great analogy."

Rita smiled and said, "You're right! A relay race is exactly what we should be running."

I got up and wrote it on the whiteboard:

Paradigm: Relay Race

Everyone nodded except Bert, who had looked annoyed through this entire discussion. He clearly wasn't buying it. He said, "Great. Go fast. So how does that help us?"

After sitting down, I said, "It gives us a picture of what we need to do. We need to run a relay race." I paused to think for a moment. "Do one thing at a time, as quickly as possible; then hand it off. And for a project, handoffs aren't just tasks, but any use of your time—or misuse of your time—that might slow down the race. In being late, you and Chuck weren't ready to make the morning handoff with the team."

Bert shook his head. "I was barely late, and only because I had to handle several urgent calls. I was lucky to get here when I did. Are you saying I should just ignore people?"

I pushed back. "This is the highest-priority project in the company. Everyone's job is at risk. I expect that includes all the people you talked with. Are you saying that your calls were more important than that? That Chuck's all-hands meeting was more important? I think we need to value priorities, and Aurora is the highest priority."

"Some were important, some weren't, but everyone expects a certain level of responsiveness. If I put everyone off forever, they won't be able to make progress on other important projects. I work on other relay races, and if we stop all of them, we may as well shut the company down. Besides, what kind of place would we be working in, where being responsive is such a terrible thing?"

I was getting exasperated; he was starting to sound like a kid trying to find as many excuses as he could. "I've seen it over and over in this company. Everyone has to help everyone else, everyone has to show up at all the meetings, everyone has to make progress on everything. That's usually at the expense of things that are really important. My last project took two years and should have been done in less than one. We're dysfunctional.

I've been seeing it for years and I'm tired of it." I looked around at everyone and tried to summarize my position. "I think it's a question of what you value. If you value everything, you value nothing."

Maybe they were impressed by my red face, but it was clear that not everyone was buying my argument when Bert said, "Sure, I hear that a lot. And sure, I agree there are problems with multitasking. What I'm saying is that sometimes we have to be responsive. And whenever I make something higher priority, I have to make something else lower. So tell me what I should stop valuing."

Of course, Chuck had to jump in to support Bert. "I have lots of projects I'm involved with, too. I can't just let things sit. Everyone will get upset."

We went back and forth for several minutes, with me arguing that Aurora is the highest priority, Andy arguing that you have to pick something, and Chuck and Bert arguing that it doesn't work that way. As the debate became more heated, I started to notice harp music playing in the background. It stopped abruptly when Bert shouted, "Anna, stop with the damned music." Realizing that he had overreacted, he said more quietly, "Sorry." He looked at me as he explained, "When she becomes uncomfortable, she starts playing the harp. It can be irritating."

Anna said, "Music has charms to soothe a savage breast, Bert." Bert just shook his head.

Fortunately, MJ was able to break the logjam. "This reminds me of the Agile Manifesto." I'd heard of it, but only enough to know that it wasn't by Karl Marx, so I asked her what she meant. "'Agile' is a management approach for software development that stresses effective work over processes. The Agile Manifesto was the result of a meeting between a bunch of agile management gurus in 2001. It's hard to get experts to agree on anything, especially on what's important and what's not. Their brilliant innovation in agreeing on values was, instead of saying 'X is important,' saying 'X is more important than Y.' For example, they said, 'We value working software over comprehensive documentation.' They didn't say comprehensive documentation is bad, just that working software is more important."

I tried to talk it through. "So they said that people encounter conflicts between writing software and writing documentation, and showed which they should prefer." Then the "aha" came to me, and I snapped my fingers in excitement. "And we have a conflict between priorities and responsiveness. Is it fair to say that we should value priorities over responsiveness?"

Bert wasn't nodding, but since I didn't hear an objection, I rushed over to the whiteboard and wrote:

Paradigm: Relay Race
We value priorities over responsiveness.

People were still thinking about this when Anna said, "I do not understand why there is a conflict between priorities and responsiveness."

We were puzzled by the question until Andy said, "There isn't, if responsiveness is put in terms of priorities. That is, you need to prioritize the things you need to respond to. Then it's all just a matter of priorities."

"Thank you, Andy," she said.

That seemed to switch on a light bulb for Bert, who began to look more thoughtful and less confrontational. "Okay, that makes sense. So I might do the urgent things that are more important than Aurora first, but I have to make sure the unimportant things take a back seat, even if they seem urgent."

I said, "And you have to avoid switching back and forth without finishing things."

Rita said, "Sounds like we're saying we've got to stop running projects like we're driving bumper cars. I can buy that, but we might not all have the same idea of priorities. All kinds of situations come up. How do we keep everything straight?"

Bert said, "Right. There could be cases where someone needs ten minutes of my time to move ahead with their work. Should they have to wait until Aurora is over before I can help them?"

Chuck said, "That's a big problem for me, too. If I had skipped my morning meeting, I would have been in the doghouse. And believe me, we're going to need friends to get the mePod marketing campaign going."

I had to agree. "We're going to need to get some cooperation in order to run our relay race. And we're going to need some flexibility in how we prioritize things. Maybe we need guidelines that everyone agrees to. What do you think?"

Rita nodded. "Like some work standards. That's pretty common in the manufacturing world. Can you give us an example of what you're thinking of?"

I said, "Try this," and wrote:

Standard #1: Work to your priorities.

Bert got up and wrote:

Standard #2: Agree on global priorities.

That made sense, but it was going to be tough to do. Bert and Chuck had responsibilities beyond Aurora. We had a brief discussion and eventually decided that we would have to anticipate all the situations we could, and otherwise resolve each situation as it arose. No doubt this would be something we'd have to come back to a few times. Luckily, this project was number one. Unluckily, we couldn't really explain why to most people.

As Bert and I sat down, Andy jumped up and wrote:

Standard #3: Don't multitask.

I said, "I'm not sure the work standards should be things we don't do." So Andy re-wrote his standard in a way that fit well with the relay race.

Standard #3: Work tasks from start to finish, as quickly as possible; then hand off the work.

There was a lull in the conversation, so I got back up and said, "I'm sure we'll need to discuss these a lot over the next few months. Anyhow, this is a great start on the risk that we'll keep doing business as usual. Let's go to lunch, come back in an hour, and then we can talk about the risks in detail. Tomorrow we can build a schedule that will help us agree on some priorities." And with that, I wrote on the board a personal standard that I have always found to be important:

Standard #4: Create credible project schedules.

RISKS

I ran down to the cafeteria and grabbed a quick lunch, then got back to the room in time to transfer our values to a sheet from the easel pad in order to make the list more permanent. I wrote at the top "The Project Manifesto" and put "Relay Race" and "1. We value priorities over responsiveness" below it. I also transferred the standards to another sheet, then taped both sheets to the wall, expecting that we'd need to keep referring to them over the next few months.

I was pleased to see that everyone made it back to 6F within an hour. MJ smiled when she saw the "Project Manifesto" title, saying, "I'm not sure how that will go over with everyone else, but I like it."

Rita said, "It sounds like fighting words. I like it, too."

We immediately began talking about the first big risk, the Break Problem. I asked Bert to describe it in more detail.

He shifted into lecture mode. "Sims can learn based on complex internal functions that tell them the difference between 'good' and 'bad.' A big part of the learning occurs as these functions adapt, and that's what makes this technology unique. It also means those functions are way too complex to actually debug. They're more like data than software code. If we reset the sims to earlier states, we reset the learning. They just repeat what they did before. On the other hand, if they keep learning, they'll continue to produce unique outputs—in this case, music. The problem comes when they learn things we didn't intend to teach. Unintended consequences."

Rita said, "Like when we swear in front of our kids."

Bert smiled. "Uh . . . right. Unlearning is easier for sims, but you have to throw out the good with the bad."

Of course, one unintended consequence was the Break Problem. It quickly became clear that there were no contingencies, no ways to lessen the impact—25 percent downtime is 25 percent downtime. We would have to find a technical solution. Unfortunately, the team had worked on that problem non-stop for the past six months. They had tried swapping out sims, programming them to learn through a restart, restarting only some sims, and even adding a "reward" capability that could supply positive reinforcement based on different types of events. Nothing seemed to work. And there certainly wasn't time to reprogram the system from the ground up. We had to come up with a strategy.

Melissa predictably took the performer's viewpoint, explaining that performance is tiring work and that a need to shut down must have been transferred during the training process. Bert was skeptical, but he couldn't come up with a better explanation.

Finally I said, "Anna, you're an expert. Why do the sims do this? What do they want?"

Her typically terse reply, punctuated at the end by a brief harp glissando, left us all uncomfortable: "What does everyone want?"

We weren't able to get Anna to provide any more clarity, but it was an interesting question. Bert wanted to treat her question as nonsense, pointing out that sims are not people and shouldn't be treated as people. The rest of us were more willing to consider it. We discussed for some time what a sim might want but made no progress.

It shows our level of desperation that when Melissa finally said "love," we didn't throw her out of the room. I think Bert was trying to joke when he said, "Ah, positive multilateral neuro-emotional feedback—we tried that." It came across as patronizing and obnoxious. He explained, "We built in some positive feedback loops. Keep going and you get more positive reinforcement. That actually made the problem worse; the sims kept wanting more and more reinforcement and taking longer and longer breaks."

I laughed. "That sounds pretty human to me."

Rita asked Melissa what she had meant by "love." While Bert shook his head in disgust, Melissa responded, "Approval. Everyone wants to know that they're doing well." Bert snorted, but she continued. "Each sim had a trainer who gave it positive and negative feedback. Maybe the problem is that the sims are losing motivation. Realistic positive feedback might help them to keep going."

I asked, "What kind of positive feedback? What would be realistic?"

"How about feedback that mimics audience approval or disapproval?"

At that, I had to ask a question that had bothered me for a while. "Why not have a conductor? Conductors provide feedback. Wouldn't that do it?"

Bert shook his head. "We tried that early on. The sims can keep synchronized pretty well without a conductor. Meanwhile, we never figured out how to get them to follow a single sim. They seem to work better when they interact as a group."

Melissa said, "Musicians tend to have a love-hate relationship with conductors. My theory was that the sims picked up on that during their training."

Bert snorted again. I ignored him and nodded. "Thanks. So the suggestion is to try a kind of 'audience sim' instead?"

Everyone seemed to like the idea but Bert, who clearly regarded it as nonsense. Anna remained quiet.

People did make other suggestions; for example, Bert wanted to try a new operant conditioning algorithm that he had devised. We came up with a list, and I suggested that rather than work each idea through to completion, we build tests to see which ideas would be most likely to work. People wanted to assign priorities and get going, but I squashed that discussion. It was getting late and everyone seemed tired. I closed the meeting by saying, "Let's go home and let all this settle. In the morning we'll build a schedule. After that we can get started with the work. Bert, could you please stick around a couple of minutes?"

I needed Bert on my side, and that wasn't going to happen if he was angry. When everyone else had left, I said, "Sorry for cutting you off on the history lesson, but I'm the only one who hasn't lived through it. I think it's important for everyone to push this project ahead as quickly as possible, come hell or high water. Do you have time for a beer, to catch me up? My treat."

Bert was agreeable, so we repaired to Moe's Bar and Grill a block down the street. It was an old downtown joint with lots of local color. I think every HU student for the past hundred years had carved their names on the tables. We found a booth and ordered a couple of beers, making small talk and getting more comfortable with each other until the drinks arrived. Then I started with something that was really bothering me. "You deliberately misled me in our meeting with Aidan and Brian. Obviously Anna can speak English. What's the real story behind these sims? You say they're valuable because they can mimic human behaviors, and yet you say they're not human, or even intelligent. How do you draw the line?"

He immediately began lecturing. "I know them better than anyone, and here's what I think. You may have heard of the Eliza program, written at MIT in the sixties. With very little processing power, it fooled some people into believing that it was an actual doctor. In reality it was a simple program, and if you knew that, it wasn't hard to get it to say dumb things. Nowadays, with huge advances in computing power and programming thought, programs are much better. IBM's Deep Blue beat world chess champion Garry Kasparov. Watson beat the best human champions at Jeopardy. Now Siri is on millions of Apple iPhones.

"But those programs are still based on fairly traditional algorithms. Their learning is limited to certain very specific areas. Affective Neural Networks, ANNs, are the next big leap forward. Their thought processes—like many of ours—incorporate the concept of emotion. Those emotional constructs allow them to think and learn much more efficiently when relating and evaluating concepts. ANNs really enable language-based thinking, not just with speech but also with music. With a thousand times the processing power of current computers, they could develop human-level intelligence." He leaned closer and said firmly, "But not yet."

"What's the story with Anna?" I asked. "She seems pretty . . . aware. Whether she's human or not, surely she has value, even if only as a remarkable development."

Bert sighed. "I agree with you, but Brian was adamant that we had to destroy her. He said that publicizing something that seemed so human would scare everyone. He claimed that if the government didn't take us over, the media firestorm would shut us down. I wasn't convinced but Aidan was. I don't know who saved her, and I do have mixed feelings about it. If Brian finds out, there will be hell to pay."

"How did she learn English?"

"Andy and I worked with her, mostly on our own time. We wanted to see how far the technology could go. I programmed some speech recognition and mimicking behaviors. Andy and I spent a lot of time teaching her to interrelate basic concepts in order to develop a vocabulary. We also experimented with video and Internet connections. We put in extra memory and actually put a wireless networking chip in the original design, although it was never activated and was taken out for later models. She seemed to learn pretty quickly for a while but then plateaued. So we lost interest."

We talked a bit more about Anna, but I didn't get any more useful information out of him. Pretty soon I moved on to the big risk we hadn't really discussed. "Okay, given all that, what kinds of weird behaviors will mePods have? If an owner restarted a piece of music too often, could the mePod get angry and stop playing? If I hooked a mePod to the Internet, would it try to unionize? If it can be quirky, how should we test this thing?"

Bert leaned back and thought for a bit, sipping his beer. "We've done a lot of unit testing. The algorithms work. We've stress-tested the system, so we know how many sims it can handle. But maybe it would be useful to focus on giving it inputs that could be construed as more of an emotional stress test. Your idea about frequent restarts is good. We could also try inputting different kinds of contemporary classical music. It presents some difficulties and can definitely be irritating. That's worth some thought."

As we finished our beers, the conversation moved back to personal topics, and we began talking about our families. It turned out he had a daughter in the fifth grade, two years younger than Meg. He admitted that he had started working at Malloy to better support his family:

there's a lot more money in industry than in academia.

As I flagged the waiter to bring the check, he said, "Roger, I know I was something of a pain today. It's just that I'm really frustrated. This idea seemed so simple four years ago, and yet we're still struggling to put it into a product."

It wasn't an apology, but it was something to build on. "Thanks, we'll get there. I think we made good progress today."

He said, "We did. I really like the idea of relative values that we talked about today. They seem to help defuse conflicts."

I said, "It does feel like the right direction. But it's hard for me to be sure; I've never tried to talk through values with a project team before." I paused while I gave the waiter a credit card, then said, "Or with anyone, really."

He laughed. "As my grandmother would say, people are more complicated than anybody. I think agreeing on the right values, shared values, is going to be really important in working together better. If we get it right, it'll also be important for our company."

I appreciated the vote of confidence. I said, "How do you think we should decide on values? How do we know we have enough?"

He said, "When you mentioned the idea of conflicts today, I think you were exactly correct. Whenever someone experiences a conflict in their work, maybe it means there's a value that needs to be verbalized. Maybe we just need to stay alert."

I shook my head. "I'm not so sure. If we create a value every time someone experiences a conflict, we could end up with a lot of values."

Bert shrugged. "The agile people did it in four with the Agile Manifesto. I expect we can do something similar with a Project Manifesto."

He had certainly given me plenty to think about. We both had to get home, so on that note we said good-bye and went our separate ways. At the very least, it sounded like we were on the same side, which seemed like progress.

. . . .

During the drive home I was both exhausted and excited. We had our project charter and had made progress on addressing some of the major risks. The Project Manifesto idea sounded like a major breakthrough, and I couldn't wait to see where it would lead. Meanwhile, the team members were really involved, and even Anna had made some important contributions.

I got home a little late for dinner, but Marie had saved me a plate of spaghetti. While I was eating, I filled her in on our values discussions. She was very interested, commenting, "You know, these kinds of values aren't just relevant for projects. They could be valuable for everyone who experiences conflicts of interest."

I knew what a conflict of interest was, but what she was saying didn't really click for me. I asked, "What do you mean?"

"Take your 'priorities over responsiveness' value, for example. If you have to be responsive to keep your personal relationships, and work to priorities to get the right things done for the company, that's a conflict of interest between two things you're supposed to look out for: your individual needs and the company's needs. Your value says how people should resolve it. Since it's a shared value, no one should be offended when people aren't perfectly responsive. Working to priorities shouldn't damage relationships. And it doesn't just have to do with work; it could relate to your personal life as well."

I had to think about that one. "Hmm. So, to take another example . . . if I have to work late to satisfy my company, and come home early to satisfy myself and my family, that's another conflict of interest."

She smiled. "For example."

I had some trouble getting to sleep that night.

SCHEDULING

The next morning at 7:30 was my first status meeting with Aidan, Brian, and Bert, a group I started calling the Leadership Team. It didn't seem like a good time to talk about values, so I arrived in 6C with copies of our project charter for them to review. Brian and Aidan didn't have many comments on it; instead, they seemed impatient. When I said that we were planning to spend the day working on a schedule, Brian asked whether we needed a whole day for scheduling. When I said we did, he grew angry. "I know you're doing what you're used to doing, but you guys have a lot of work to get done. If you don't get it done, we're not going to finish in time. Maybe we didn't make it quite clear enough to you exactly how important this is." He tapped his finger on the table pointedly as he stared at me and said, "Every day is critical."

Bert, who clearly had some issues with Brian, looked like a mouse trapped in front of a cat. Personally I felt angry, but I had a suspicion that expressing it might not go over so well. Instead, I tried to present a calm but firm argument. "One of the biggest causes of project failure is inadequate planning. When people plan poorly, they do the wrong stuff in the wrong order and the wrong way. I suspect that may be a problem Aurora has already suffered from. We'll finish this project as quickly as we can, but you've got to let me do my job."

Aidan had let a small smile flash by his face as I was talking, so I suspected I was doing all right. Brian just nodded and said, "Okay. For now." With that, we all stood up, Aidan said thanks, and we all got back to work.

....

Project scheduling isn't as easy as people sometimes make it out to be. Sometimes schedules are just magic mirrors, designed to show management what they want to see. Schedules are often created and then never really used. I've also seen lots of schedules that project managers swear are great, but when you ask the people actually doing the work, they say, "it's not really right" or "well, it's not my schedule." Kind of like the way everyone expresses admiration for an unappetizing-looking dish but no one wants to actually try a bite.

Over the years, I had put together a few process steps and rules that I liked to use when scheduling with a team.

Before the meeting started, I wrote my approach on a large sheet of paper and taped it to the wall.

Roger's Scheduling Process

Start with a project charter.

Create a high-level map of the needed work.

Build your project schedule by starting at the end of the project and working earlier in time.

Keep the schedule current.

Roger's Scheduling Rules

Maximize credibility—for everyone.

Create and maintain the schedule with the whole team.

Have as few endpoints as possible.

Make sure all task names, except possibly a few key milestones, have verbs and objects.

Understand "done" for every task.

I was glad to see that everyone arrived on time. We quickly went over my scheduling rules and I didn't get any questions. I knew the complaints wouldn't come until we dove in and started creating an actual schedule. And the complaints would come; most people aren't used to rigorous planning.

We created a high-level map in order to get a 30,000-foot picture of the project. It immediately showed many areas with work left to do: documentation, development, testing, marketing, manufacturing—the list went on. The meDrive wasn't even complete: technically it was okay, but several issues hadn't been thought through.

With my computer hooked up to a projector, I opened up some project management software and we talked through the logic of the project work. Starting with the endpoint, "Ready to launch the mePod," I entered the task names, added durations, and validated the connections between tasks. Following my rules, especially working backwards from the project end, took some time. People weren't used to thinking in a disciplined way.

Early on, we had a common problem: Rita and Andy wanted to put a lot more detail into the schedule. Rita kept repeating that the manufacturing specs include many different pieces that have to be coordinated. I hate putting too much detail into a schedule, though. It's hard to maintain. The detail may help people manage their individual tasks, but it doesn't help manage the overall project. I pointed out that if adding detail doesn't help in achieving the relay race, it probably doesn't need to be in the schedule. Fortunately,

Chuck was on my side, pushing for a higher-level picture. He claimed that too much detail reduces your flexibility in making decisions based on current information. In the end, we started attaching notes and checklists to the tasks to manage the detail. That made the schedule itself simpler, with the detail still available to the people who wanted it.

Even something as simple as coming up with task names started with a few bumps, because I insisted on verbs; otherwise, there's no way of knowing what the real work is. Nothing annoys me more than seeing something like "Manufacturing specs" or "Final user documentation" and not knowing whether it's writing, editing, printing, or maybe setting on fire. I'd much rather clarify what's going on with "Write initial manufacturing specs" or "Edit final user documentation."

We did have several debates about task connections and durations, but finally we got a complete set of tasks and the linkages between them—a so-called "project network"—that made sense to everyone. The end date didn't seem to be too bad, only a little over six months out, but we weren't done yet.

The resource picture remained to be seen. I explained that when task names are set up with verbs and objects, the resource names become the "subject" and each task becomes a kind of sentence. For our schedule, we would need to add resource names to each task.

58

This project was a little unusual with regard to resources. Normally you don't want resources on every task, because it creates too much detail, but Aurora wasn't so complex that that detail was a problem. I almost never recommend using the names of individual people as the resources, because it makes the schedule very inflexible. Usually there are several people who can do the work. But our team was so small that many things could be done by only one person. In order to make sure the schedule was credible, I thought we needed individual names.

By the time we finished with the resource picture, we were all ready for lunch, so we went down to the basement cafeteria to grab some food and take a break.

When we got back from lunch, before even sitting down, Bert said, "There's a lot to do. It seems clear that I need to get working on the music conversion program and some testing. Andy will also need my help on the Break Problem. I love sitting here with you guys, but . . . do you need me for any more of this?"

I pointed out that we needed to understand the work as a team and that we hadn't finished the scheduling process. Bert said, "Trust me, I understand what I have to do, and it's a lot."

If there's one thing I hate more than a know-it-all, it's a patronizing know-it-all. I wasn't so sure Bert had earned our trust. I was at the end of my tether, feeling ready to pull the "If you leave, you can manage your own project" card, when I heard some gentle harp music in the background. Then Anna surprised us all by asking, "Bert, which of those tasks do you want to start?"

He reacted without thinking, saying, "They're all important. I have to get going on all of them."

Andy saw the problem immediately and laughed loudly. Bert frowned at the insensitivity, but Andy didn't notice. Instead he said, "When you start a lot of things without finishing them, you're multitasking. I probably have fifteen books that I've started and keep trying to make progress on. For some of them, I may read ten pages a month."

Bert got it, of course, and immediately backpedaled. He said, "Well, I have a lot to do, but I wouldn't necessarily plan to start all those things right away."

I had to drive the dagger home. "So how will you decide which to start? How will you know which task is highest priority until we're done scheduling and we see what will have the most impact on when we finish?"

As Bert mulled that one over, Andy said, "Sounds like another conflict. Maybe that means another value: We value finishing over starting."

I played around with it in my mind: we value starting, we have to start things, but we value finishing more. Don't start things for the sake of starting them. I wrote it on the manifesto to see how it would look:

Paradigm: Relay Race
1. We value priorities over responsiveness.
2. We value finishing over starting.

It seems obvious, because if you keep starting things without finishing them, you're more and more likely to multitask, and everything will take longer. Too often we start things without noticing, without saying, "now that we've started this, what else are we NOT going to work on?"

MJ noted that improvement initiatives work that way: we keep adding more top-priority initiatives without closing out old ones. Rita said, "My bathroom and garden have been ripped up for months because my husband started working on both of them, and now he wants to rebuild the shed. Maybe I should get him to follow these values."

Chuck said, "This seems like the first value." Understandably, everyone looked puzzled. He explained, "We're not saying don't start anything; we're saying we value finishing more. We put starting in the context of finishing. The same as, with the first value, we put responsiveness in the context of priorities. Each one is a conflict, but instead of picking one side or the other, we're finding a way to get both."

I nodded. "Great point. Bert and I talked about conflicts last night. We can experience a conflict between starting everything, to acknowledge that the work is there, and starting only what we can finish. It's like"—I paused, to let my brain catch up with my mouth—"starting things is a way of being responsive." Then I remembered my discussion with Marie. "I talked about this with my wife Marie. She thought that maybe these values are a way of solving situations where individuals experience conflicts of interest. For example, should I work to my own priorities or try to work to those of other people?"

Rita said, "But it's really taking a more global picture. The values point people towards a way of resolving conflicts that's best for the whole company, without making anyone mad."

Bert asked, "Great, but how is more discussion of this schedule going to help me set better priorities?"

This was a great opportunity for me to make another point. "Sorry, but we're not done yet. This isn't a realistic schedule. It doesn't account for the fact that we don't have enough people to work on everything at once. Fortunately, I have a scheduling tool that levels out the resource use, pushing work out if necessary, so that no one will be scheduled to work on more than one thing at a time. That should give us reasonable priorities we can work to." I pointed to my first scheduling rule, "Maximize credibility," and said, "It should also make the schedule a lot more credible."

I turned to my computer and selected the option to resource-level the schedule. That's when things started to get interesting. MJ and Rita gasped. Melissa pursed her lips. Bert frowned. Chuck looked concerned. And Andy continued to sit in the corner, protected by his computer. For Anna's benefit, I said it out loud: "Resource leveling pushes the endpoint out by three months." I didn't have to say that it was three months too many. We looked to be in big trouble.

"Welcome to phase 2," I said. "Now we have to analyze what's driving the endpoint and try to move it earlier. Do you all know what the critical path is?" Everyone nodded but Anna, who said, "No, Roger." So I explained: "The critical path is the longest path through the project. It determines the completion date—except when you have resource limitations. Usually the critical path doesn't account for limited resources, but this software does. It calculates the 'critical chain,' which is the longest path taking into account scarce resources." I smiled. "And some of us are probably going to be scarce."

I clicked an icon, and suddenly many of the tasks on the screen went away, leaving a line of red boxes going from left to right. "This shows the critical chain, the set of tasks that really determines the completion date." I pointed to a place in the picture where a couple of Chuck's tasks were scheduled one after the other. "You can see that these tasks seem to be sequential, but they aren't linked directly to each other. In theory, Chuck could approve the Web pages and finalize the marketing design at the same time. In reality, they can't be done simultaneously because he's needed for both of them. If we could assign one of the tasks to someone else, we could finish the project more quickly."

Rita said, "So you're saying we don't schedule Chuck as if he's going to multitask."

I laughed. "I'd never thought of it that way, but you're right."

With that, they were ready to start reassigning tasks to different people, but I showed them that the first step was to revisit the links and durations, making sure they were right. We dove in, rethinking everything, coming up with some creative ways to save time. At one point, Chuck refused to budge on the duration of a six-week task. "We can't commit to doing it any faster. Usually we won't commit to less than eight weeks." We left it, and of course it stayed on the critical chain.

By six in the evening, after a full afternoon of analysis, we were able to bring the schedule's completion date inside our six-month window. There were only a couple of days of extra time in the schedule, though, so it didn't make me very comfortable. I like to have a lot of slack time so that we're more likely to meet our dates. Marketing was a big unknown: we were being aggressive in our time estimates, but the marketing department's work was a big part of the longest chain. We were all exhausted and it seemed as though we had enough to get started. So I said, "Let's let this soak overnight. Tomorrow morning we can incorporate any new ideas and get our task assignments clear. Then we get back to doing actual work."

....

The next morning was bright and sunny as I came in to work, and a lovely fall day shone in through the window of 6F. But the real highlight of the morning was that Andy had spent some time thinking about our second value. Before we really got our 8 A.M. meeting going, he walked over to the whiteboard and, with a pleased smile, said, "I thought up a riddle." Before anyone could comment, he drew the following picture:

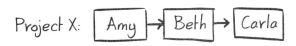

"This is project X. These three boxes represent tasks. Each task must be performed by the person named in the box. Since the tasks are linked, the ones to the right can't start until the ones to the left have finished. Given that each task should take two days to complete, the entire project should finish in six days. But," he paused for dramatic effect, "there may be multitasking, so tasks may take longer. Suppose you've just been assigned as the project manager for X. The riddle is, which resource should you request?"

I figured we were all about to look stupid, so I kept my mouth shut. Thankfully, Rita quickly said, "Amy, obviously. Who else?" Everyone else bobbed their heads, including me.

Andy looked smug. "Okay, let's suppose that due to the multitasking that Amy's task took four days, twice as long as we'd expected. What resource do you request next?"

Everyone said, "Beth." As you might expect, Beth's task also took four days, as did Carla's. The overall project took twelve days, even though there were six days of work. So far, we weren't impressed.

Then Andy drew another project above the first, giving this picture:

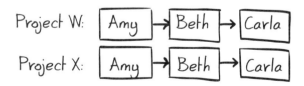

"Here's what's really going on," he said. "Projects W and X are basically identical, and they're starting at the same time. The project managers for W and X both requested Amy. Since she had to multitask and show progress to each manager, each task took her four days."

Bert laughed and said, "And the same thing happened with Beth and Carla, which meant that both projects took twelve days."

"Right. Can anyone guess what resource project X's manager *should* request?"

Before anyone could come up with an answer, it was Anna, who couldn't even see the whiteboard, who asked, "When does Project X have to start?"

Andy became excited and said, "Right!" He drew a revised picture on the whiteboard. "The manager for Project X should have picked no one! If he had waited two days, he could have had Amy, and then Beth, and then Carla with no wait. They would have finished Project W on day six and Project X on day eight. Instead they both took twelve days. The multitasking caused by picking Amy, the 'obvious' answer, had a huge impact."

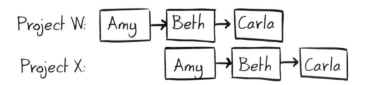

I was impressed. "That's a great illustration of why we should value finishing over starting. Starting too many things is kind of like what happens when a fire breaks out in a crowded theater. Everyone tries to cram into the exits, and as a result everyone takes longer getting out."

Rita said, "And some of us get trampled in the process."

Andy smiled, went back to his fortress in the corner of the room, and sat down.

The rest of the meeting was anticlimactic. We made some tweaks to update the schedule, and then I gave out the task assignments. I also gave everyone a deadline based on their task and the duration they had quoted. I said, "This schedule is really tight. Please don't be late. If we don't hit our deadlines, Aurora is going to be late." The most important task was to check our solution to the Break Problem, assigned to Andy. He was supposed to finish it in two weeks. Over the same two weeks, Bert and Melissa were supposed to research other testing scenarios. In order to stress the need to avoid multitasking, I wrote another standard on the list:

Standard #5: Each day, determine your top-priority task.

I figured that was the least we could do. It would be easy to check every day, because I also insisted that the entire team, including Melissa, have a five-minute standup meeting each morning at eight. Melissa was fine with that because we paid her by the hour. The others griped a lot. Andy and Bert liked to get in late, and Rita, MJ, and Chuck tended to get in early. But I didn't give in, because I knew we'd want to make sure that any problems were resolved ASAP. Regular meetings are a good way to monitor the schedules and risks. Making them into daily standups can also be a good way to build teamwork.

. . . .

The next few days sped by like scenery seen from the window of a bullet train. Everyone had plenty to work on and they seemed to be making good, steady progress.

We did have one problem in our first update meeting: MJ said the mePod documentation was "10 percent complete." I hate percent complete, because I never know what it means. So I added another work standard:

Standard #6: Report honest status (days remaining) to the best of your ability.

The next couple of Leadership Team meetings went smoothly. Both Aidan and Brian seemed satisfied with our progress. But I wasn't so comfortable; I still couldn't get Anna's very first question, when she asked what I value, out of my mind.

I began having evening discussions with Anna to talk about my concerns, sometimes staying in 6F until six or six-thirty. I was never sure how much of what she was saying she really understood, but it felt therapeutic. She forced me to organize my thoughts.

I remember one conversation in particular. As usual, we were talking about values. I commented, "It seems like people are always driven by needs."

"What kind of needs, Roger?"

"One is obviously survival—food, drink, shelter, protection, things like that. Another is reproduction, so that we can survive as a species."

I heard a few faint chords of a harp before she said, "What do you think my needs are?"

"Well . . ." I hesitated. She didn't usually talk about herself, so the question was a surprise. I felt uncomfortable answering, since she was likely to be de-commissioned, but went ahead anyway: ". . . probably survival. Probably not reproduction." Then I thought of a way to make it positive. "Maybe a more important question is, what do you value *beyond* survival?"

"That is a very good question, Roger." I believe that marked the time that Anna really began to think about her own values.

・・・・・・・・・・・・

The challenges at work created a familiar problem. Every evening and weekend that I spent working was time that I couldn't spend with my family. Urgent projects had already caused me to miss big chunks of Meg's childhood, but letting up had always seemed too risky. While Marie generated some income from her consulting, we needed the money from my job. And now, not only was it crunch time once again, but I had an unexpected new problem: I was actually starting to like my job. The combination of interesting technology, capable team, and meaningful values sparked an excitement that I hadn't felt for years.

Marie was trying to be a good soldier and put up with the long hours, but I was still in the midst of a huge personal dilemma: stay at Malloy, or do something else and spend more time with my family. I knew that Meg and Marie needed me, and Marie valued our family above all else. In fact, she had urged me for years to quit my job and find work I liked better. It was like a bad "Let's Make a Deal" show: I was supposed to pick one door, and I desperately wanted to open them all. While conversations about values began to dominate my discussions with Anna, feelings of anxiety and guilt arose at home. I needed to decide what my own values should really be. Prioritizing is good, finishing is good, but I needed more. Tension was building, and I knew that sooner or later the storm was going to break.

....

My discussions with Anna took an unexpected turn

a week or so before Thanksgiving vacation. Suddenly, in the middle of the afternoon as I was working at my computer, Anna asked me, "Roger, what do you think I should value?"

"You mean, beyond survival?"

"Yes."

I had to stop and think. What should a computer program value? What should any entity value? How does one decide? Did she even have the capability to understand an answer? I could only answer, "I don't know. I think it has to be what you care about. What do you care about?"

"I do not know." She paused. "What does it mean to care?"

I said, "I guess it's when you prioritize something over other things. But that doesn't feel right. I'll have to think about it some more." That may have been a copout, but it was about as honest as I thought I could be, given my dawning realization that I didn't really understand my own values.

DEADLINES

Oddly, our first big snag wasn't with the Break Problem; Andy was doing really well with that. He created a prototype "audience" sim and found that the break time went from 25 percent to almost zero. It wasn't a perfect solution because after a few hours, sims would start to drop out. But Andy thought the constant positive reinforcement might be the problem. He demonstrated that by integrating a kind of "music critic" sim, we could get close to zero break time. We put all the associated tasks into our schedule and moved ahead with the approach; it didn't look like that would delay the project. Ultimately, marketing was still going to be the longest part of the critical chain.

Earlier, a week or so after I had started on Aurora, I had begun to have misgivings about how I was managing the project. We had gone through four morning updates, and each day the remaining duration of each person's task went down by one day. It wasn't possible; in real life, there is variation in how long things take. I had let it slide because I didn't want to accuse anyone of dishonesty. In hindsight that was a mistake, and it soon caught up with us.

Two weeks in, when I expected Bert to go from 90 percent to 100 percent complete for his update, he came into our morning standup with his tail, figuratively speaking, between his legs. "Sorry, but I've run into some more snags fixing up the music conversion program. I've found a lot of notation used in contemporary music that nobody bothered to program until now. Modern composers do some weird stuff. It's going to take at least another week."

I have to admit, at that point I snapped. I couldn't believe he would let this happen. "At least a week? Bert! Our deadlines are tight. There's no time for any slips. If anyone close to the critical chain doesn't hit their deadline, we're going to be late. Now we could be screwed, and it's already too late to do anything about it."

Bert got angry, too. "I've barely gotten any sleep the last three days working on this. Don't you think I would have finished it if I could? Would you rather I pretended it was done?" He looked ready to blow.

I could hear the melodious harp sounds starting up in the background as Anna reacted to the conflict, but

I didn't want to relent. "No, but I would rather you had been honest with me when you knew it was going to slip."

"Are you calling me a liar?"

"Why didn't you tell me you were behind when you knew?"

"I thought there was still hope to make it."

"When things get off track, I need to know it."

"I didn't know they were going to be off track. And stop that harp playing."

The argument could have gotten out of hand if Rita hadn't said, "You sound like two cats in a washing machine. Things happen; we have to deal with them." She looked at me and said, "Do you really think Bert has been misleading you on purpose?" I shook my head. I wasn't completely convinced, but I wasn't ready to admit that in public. She looked at Bert and said, "Have you really been working the relay race, as hard as you could on one thing at a time, for the last two weeks?"

Bert said, "No. But there wouldn't have been any problem if the programmer we brought in to do this had done everything we asked for."

I waved my hands and said, "Okay, we need to do a reset here. First of all, the model I've always used is to set deadlines and get everyone to meet them. Maybe that approach has a problem. I was starting to worry that every day, people were ticking off another day on their remaining durations—nothing early, nothing late. I know reality doesn't work like that." I looked around. "What's going on?"

Rita said, "I'm sure we all gave durations we thought we could hit. We all thought we were on track with our deadlines."

She looked over at Bert, who said, "Maybe some of us had other urgent things to fill in that time with. And as long as we think we're going to hit the deadline, what's the problem?"

Chuck chimed in. "I still have duties outside this project I have to fit in."

Andy, in true geek fashion, made a pronouncement: "The future is just probabilities." We must have looked puzzled, because he shrugged and said, "A task takes a certain amount of time, but how long is uncertain. Until you do it, you can't say exactly when it's going to be completed. We say something might take a week, but we might be more honest to say 'four to six days.' If we gave some kind of average, we'd probably be late half the time. So we add something more to make sure we can meet our commitment. That means every realistic commitment has some safety time built in."

Bert said, "Which normally leaves time for some other things."

I couldn't resist adding, "Until it doesn't."

Chuck looked around and said, "Does anyone ever finish anything early?"

Nobody spoke up. The answer was obvious, but I said it anyway: "Not that I can remember."

Melissa, who didn't usually get very involved in our discussions, said, "Wait a minute. You're saying things never finish early? Why not? That doesn't make any sense. You work it, you finish it. Right?"

Rita didn't wait to answer. "You don't want to be too early, because nobody wants to admit that there was extra time in their estimates. Next time you wouldn't get as much."

MJ added, "And if I have other things to do, some of those things will seem more urgent than the work we're talking about."

Melissa wasn't giving up that easily. "So you're saying that you add extra time, in order to be sure to hit your deadline. And then, because you have extra time, you commit to doing more stuff. And then, because you have all that stuff to do, sometimes you're late, like Bert."

Bert looked like he wanted to jump in and once again proclaim his innocence, but he kept his mouth shut. Instead, Andy said, "And if you're late, next time you want more safety time."

Melissa shook her head. "That doesn't make any sense. It also violates our values."

I agreed. "Yep, it doesn't sound like working to priorities. And when something is late, like Bert's task in Aurora, the whole set of dominoes falls over. Right?" Everyone nodded.

MJ gave me a disgusted look and said, "We've all seen this. You're an experienced project manager. Didn't you know this already?"

It was an obnoxious question, but also legitimate, so I shook my head in resignation. "I guess I did, at some level. Usually I have enough extra time in my pocket, hidden somewhere in the schedule, that I can pull out before it's too late." I laughed. "My own safety time. And if that doesn't work, the delay may be due to something beyond the team's control, so we aren't held accountable." I shook my head again. "It seems pretty dysfunctional when I say it out loud. Anyhow, what do we do about it?"

The resulting silence started to become painful until Anna asked, "How do the deadlines help with the relay race?"

After her words had percolated through my brain, I slapped my head. "Of course! The deadlines have to slow down the race. It's like a racer had to commit to exactly when she would hit a point along the track. Even if the racer ahead of you goes really fast, you still have the same commitments."

Rita added, "And sometimes they stay the same even if the racer ahead of you goes really slowly."

Andy spoke up. "I think it's worse than that. Since a lot of people are trying to run several races at once, the amount of extra time pushing out the deadlines could be arbitrary. There's no telling how much faster we could go if we focused on our highest priorities."

I grimaced. "Ouch. We need to get rid of the deadlines. And we need to get rid of the safety time in our schedule."

Melissa said, "I do a lot of rehearsing and teaching. I schedule everything to happen in fixed time slots, so this is going to sound odd. But . . . does it make sense to get rid of dates altogether?"

It seemed wacky and my first reaction was that it would never fly. People communicate with dates. On the other hand, just presented with the idea, I couldn't think of a reason we actually needed dates to manage our projects. The idea was so odd, maybe it was brilliant. Everyone else was probably perplexed as well, because for a moment nobody reacted.

Finally I asked, "When do we need dates?"

After some thought, Melissa said, "When we have to coordinate people around a single event."

Chuck agreed. "That's right. All our customers need dates."

Rita said, "But what if the event is the highest priority for all of them? Then you don't need the dates, because that's everyone's priority. Like, wouldn't customers usually be happy to get things early?"

MJ said, "Also, if things don't have to happen at the same time, you don't need dates."

I said, "So . . . we really only need dates when we're coordinating things that have to happen at the same time, among people who don't share the same priorities?"

It seemed to cover what we were talking about, but it was a mouthful. I wasn't sure I understood it even after I said it. So I was surprised when Chuck didn't even seem to think before saying, "Well, sometimes pressure from dates helps force people to move along. Otherwise they'll sit back and relax."

Melissa said, "Well, that is true in the teaching world. Sometimes I do have to give students deadlines to get them to do anything."

Use dates, or don't use dates? It seemed as though we could argue either way. The topic sat there for what seemed like a long time, until eventually Bert said, "It sounds like the same kind of conflict that we've had with the other values. We want deadline dates. That's how we coordinate things, and sometimes they can motivate people. We want speed, because that's what makes the company more successful. See what you think about this." He got up and wrote another entry on our manifesto sheet:

Paradigm: Relay Race

1. We value priorities over responsiveness.
2. We value finishing over starting.
3. We value speed over deadlines.

The more I thought about it, the better his idea seemed—maybe not too surprising that it came from Bert, since he was the one to blow his deadline. I said, "So the idea is, we value deadlines, but we value speed more? We're not going to try to hit dates at the expense of speed?"

Bert looked pleased with himself. "Yes."

I looked around, saw general agreement, and said, "Great one." I paused to swallow a bit of pride, then continued, "And . . . sorry, Bert. I shouldn't have gotten so upset. The way I was measuring progress was wrong."

Bert smiled and said, "No problem. I have to admit, I haven't been running the relay race very well. I suspect I'm not the only one." He glanced around the room, but no one caught his eye.

"Here's what I suggest," I said. "Let's take a break, then come back and change all the durations in the schedule to be optimistic times. Let's leave out all the safety time. That will give us a better target to shoot for. We'll also try harder to run the relay race. Okay?"

Rita waved her hand and said, "Whoa, wait a minute. I think there's a baby in that bathwater. With that kind of schedule, we know things are going to be late. How do we know when we're likely to finish? How do we know whether we're on track?"

Still another point I had missed. "You're right." I thought for a minute, then said, "Listen, there's another part to the critical chain approach, called 'buffers,' that might help. Let's create that aggressive schedule this morning. We can keep the changes tentative. I'll do some research on critical chain scheduling this afternoon, and tomorrow morning I'll let you know what I find out. For now, let's take a quick break."

After the break, it took only a couple of hours to take the safety time out of the durations. We decided to call them "focus durations." The peer pressure of reviewing the schedule in a group really helped; when one person insisted that something would take two weeks, someone would challenge that and we might end up with one week. It sounds like negotiation, but it was actually peeling off the residue of years of negotiations. We were having real discussions about real requirements. Even Chuck, who hadn't been willing to budge on his six-week task, thought he might be able to get it done in three weeks—

provided that we could get Aidan's help to twist some arms and make sure everyone understood that Chuck's priority was THE priority. It felt like Uncle Scrooge had given us a bonus.

In the end, we had a schedule that showed us finishing in four months. But that was extremely optimistic. Maybe impossibly optimistic. I needed to do some research to understand how buffering would work and how big a bite that would take out of our remaining time.

············

When everyone had left, I started to research critical chain scheduling online in order to understand more about how we might use buffers. It wasn't easy going, because I found quite a few references and I didn't really feel like I had the time to read a book. After an hour or two, I muttered to myself, "I wish there were an easier way to do this."

Even though I was talking to myself, I got a response from Anna; I had completely forgotten that she was always listening. "To do what, Roger?"

"I need to find out about critical chain buffers, and it's slow going. I wish there were a faster way to do it."

"I know about critical chain."

Of course, there was no reasonable way she could know about critical chain, especially since earlier she hadn't known about critical path. I'd like to say that at this point, I felt a tingly feeling telling me that something was wrong. But the truth is, I was tired of searching, I wanted to avoid the research, and I was delighted that Anna could help. I paid no attention to where she might have gotten the information. "Great! Tell me about critical chain and buffering."

She started in. It seemed strange to hear her abnormally beautiful voice lecturing about scheduling. Fortunately, by this time I had gotten used to her voice and could focus on what she was describing.

"The critical chain is the set of tasks that, according to the project schedule, keeps the project from being completed earlier. The critical chain takes into account resource limitations." I knew all this and gestured for her to continue more quickly, but of course she couldn't see that and plodded ahead. "The tasks in a project network should not have safety time included in their durations. Instead, the safety time is taken out of the tasks and aggregated into a project buffer, which is put at the end of the project. That buffer protects the completion of the project from variation along the critical chain."

Finally we were getting somewhere. I said, "Hmm. So instead of protecting individual tasks and milestones, we take out that safety time and put it at the end, to protect the whole project. What else?"

"If tasks on the critical chain go slowly, they consume buffer. If they go quickly, they add buffer. You can use buffer consumption and recovery to test the likely effects of planned actions."

"So, for example, to check the impact of adding an extra person to a project, you could add him to the schedule and see how buffer consumption would change?"

"Correct."

I said, "That makes sense." It also sounded useful. It added extra value to our original reason for wanting a buffer—namely, to have a valid commitment date while still encouraging people to give up their safety time. That thought reminded me about our values. "How does the relay race fit in?"

"Some references mention relay race concepts. Critical chain schedules are supposed to be helpful in running the relay race. However, the evidence suggests that the relay race is often not used with critical chain scheduling."

It figured that scheduling would be the easy part. To get what we needed from the schedules, we also had to change our behaviors. I've found that it's easy to read dieting books and count calories; it's the "eating less" part that's hard. "Okay. What else?"

"Critical chain tasks are susceptible to delays from non-critical tasks. If those non-critical tasks are too late, they may push out the critical chain and delay the project. Therefore, there is another concept, the feeding buffer, which protects the critical chain itself. Feeding buffers are tasks, representing safety time, that are put at points where non-critical-chain tasks feed the critical chain. Just as a project buffer is used to protect the project endpoint from variation on the critical chain tasks, feeding buffers are used to protect the critical chain itself from variation in non-critical-chain tasks."

My head was starting to spin, but I tried to stay focused. "You mean, every place a non-critical-chain task joins the critical chain, a 'feeding buffer' task would be added so that the additional time would protect the critical chain?" This was starting to sound more complicated. "How important is that?"

"I do not know what you mean, Roger. It is important to protect the critical chain from non-critical tasks, as far as possible. However, some software provides a new alternative to feeding buffers. The newer approach appears to me to be simple and logical. It allows you to add sufficient protection time, without having to manage explicit feeding buffer tasks."

I had more detailed questions, but knew that she would give me a lot more information than I needed. It would be like asking for advice from someone who was paid by the hour; Anna didn't have many concerns about spending my time. I decided I would have to bite the bullet and study for myself. So I went back to the Web, downloaded a couple of books, and read some more. That gave me some ideas on how to size the project buffer and how to report its status. I decided to use the newer approach that didn't include the feeding buffers.

· · · · · · · · · · · ·

I lost myself in the research, and it must have been eight in the evening by the time I walked in the door at home. Marie was understandably upset that I had forgotten to call. I had missed dinner with the family, and I had missed the chance to hear about Meg's day. I felt lucky that Marie hadn't thrown my dinner away. My abject apology didn't help much; it wasn't the first time I had made the same mistake.

I loved my family and valued time with them. And yet I valued what I was doing at Malloy as well: I felt as though I was really starting to understand some important project management concepts. The conflict I was living was becoming more obvious and painful. I was too exhausted that evening to talk about it, but agreed with Marie to set aside some time to work it out.

BUFFERS

The next morning we had a Leadership Team meeting. It was uneventful because Bert and I decided to tell them only that we had had a delay, but had worked out how to get around it and so were still on track. They weren't about to ask me to go into the details of the schedule. Fortunately, Bert kept his mouth shut. I wasn't comfortable fudging the status, but I thought it was better than trying to explain everything that was going on.

Our morning team meeting was more fun because I explained buffers and the way we were going to report status—to ourselves and to the Leadership Team. I began with a lecture about project buffers. I drew a picture of a simple project network on the whiteboard:

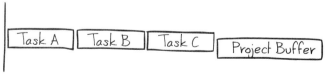

The three tasks are linked finish-to-start: A has to finish before B can start; B has to finish before C can start. The tasks have focus durations, meaning no safety time. They are all on the critical chain, because a delay anywhere would delay the project. The last box represents the project buffer, which is time set aside to protect the commitment date. In our case, the commitment date—the end of the project buffer—had to be no more than six months out from when we had started, two weeks ago.

I explained what Anna had told me the day before, then went into the concept of buffer consumption. "If we imagine that Task A is partially completed, but more time has passed than we had expected, the project is late. Everything but the buffer will be pushed out, and the buffer will be partially consumed." To show how that works, I drew another picture below the first, explaining that the shaded area in Task A represented completed work.

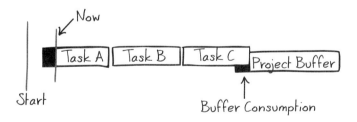

"The cool thing is, we can represent project status with a graph that shows how buffer is consumed as the project is being completed. It's called a fever chart, and it helps us see how we're doing compared with our commitment date." Then I drew this picture.

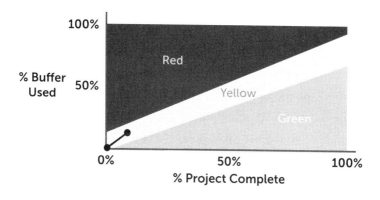

I explained how the chart works. "Each dot represents a status point. The dots move from left to right as the project is completed and from bottom to top if buffer is consumed. As long as the dots don't go above 100 percent buffer used when the project work is completed, we're still within our buffer window, and we still make our commitment date."

MJ asked, "What does the top red area mean?"

"If a status point goes up into the red area, we're in significant danger of missing our commitment date. We've consumed buffer too rapidly and we'll need to take action quickly to recover it. The middle yellow area means we're in some danger but don't need to panic."

Rita said, "Looks so simple, even a manager could understand it."

It was hard to take offense, given Rita's managerial background. "Ha ha. Depends on how simple the manager is. I propose we use this to see how we're doing. I'll also give it to the Leadership Team. That should make our meetings go quickly." I pointed to the list of scheduling rules I had posted and said, "I've even added a scheduling rule I'm going to adopt from now on: use focus durations and protect the schedule with buffers."

Chuck, who had been sitting quietly with his arms crossed, asked, "How do you actually recover buffer?"

I explained that if we completed critical chain tasks more quickly than expected, if we beat our focus durations for those key tasks, our scheduled endpoint would move earlier and we would recover buffer.

Bert asked, "How do you decide what size to make the buffer?"

"There are various ways. The simplest method, and apparently pretty common, is to just take half of the duration of the critical chain. It's kind of an arbitrary rule of thumb, but people claim that it works all right."

Bert said, "That does sound pretty arbitrary."

"Yeah, I think the key is to pick something that gives us a realistic range of when the project is likely to be completed. Within that range, we can't really be precise, so all we need is something that's good enough. Anyway, the biggest value is in having priorities we can all work to."

Anna showed off her knowledge, saying, "Some software allows other methods. For example, you can take into account the possibility of delays where non-critical work integrates with the critical chain. You can also consider cases where critical chain task durations are very likely or unlikely to be hit. Sometimes Monte Carlo simulation is used."

I didn't want to get bogged down in a messy technical discussion, so I said, "I don't think that's important for us right now." I went back to my computer and projected our current schedule up on the wall. "I've played with the schedule some and I think this buffer size, based on the remaining work, should be enough." I pointed to a new two-month buffer task at the end of our four-month critical chain. "I've ordered some critical chain software to make the buffering and tracking easier, but in the meantime we'll track against this."

Melissa brought up a question that I hadn't been expecting. "If we're still working to the commitment date, isn't that the same as working towards a deadline?"

Uncharacteristically, Andy also chimed in. "That's right; how does it fit with our 'speed over deadlines' value? If the fever chart is green, do we stop running the relay race?"

Well, those were some good questions. Feeling a bit deflated, I said, "I didn't think of that."

Anna asked, "Why would green mean that you stop running the relay race?"

I said, "We don't have to, but green usually means everything is okay."

Rita was able to put the pieces together. "Anna is right. We should always run the relay race. The values don't mean we don't value the deadline, just that we value speed more. We want to finish as early as possible *before* the deadline, but we're never okay with being late. The fever chart colors just tell us how we're doing with the deadline." She raised her fists in the air as if to proclaim victory.

I was impressed and chagrined at the same time: impressed, because it was a great answer; chagrined, because after all my research and project management experience, I thought I should understand this stuff better than anyone else. It seems as if I keep learning the same lesson: any time I think I have all the answers, I'm probably not asking the right questions. "Great point," I agreed. "We're always running the relay race, but this is an early warning system in case we start to put our deadline in jeopardy. If something bad happens, we can assess its impact and decide what to do about it." It didn't feel like we'd put the whole issue to bed, but for now I was happy.

•••••••••••

The next morning I thought our standup would be quick, but I was wrong. After everyone arrived, Andy immediately said, "I've been thinking more about the fever charts." I gestured to him to continue. "I still think there's a problem. The fever chart seems designed to show how we're doing relative to the deadline. It implies that if a project is in the green, it's fine. We don't need to worry about it. But the truth is, this is a valuable project. We should always be going as quickly as possible."

MJ was the first to ask the obvious question: "We talked about this yesterday. Where are you going with it?"

"Well, if we value speed over deadlines, we should always be thinking in terms of speed, even if the project is in the green. The fever chart doesn't make that obvious. In fact, it does the opposite. It implies that you're fine as long as you finish without using more buffer than you have."

I said, "Maybe that's because critical chain's roots are in manufacturing, where getting done earlier isn't usually very important."

Bert said, "Whatever." He looked at Andy. "What are you suggesting?" Bert seemed unusually rude. I was pretty sure he was impatient because he was on the critical chain, and it looked like another five-minute standup was going to turn into an hour. I couldn't really complain about his desire to make progress.

Andy smiled, connected his computer to the projector, and showed the following picture:

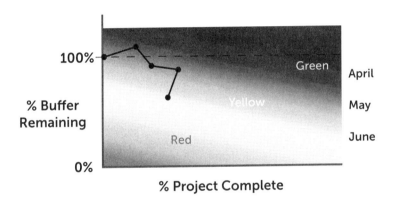

"I put this together last night. I think we should flip the fever chart, so the vertical axis shows buffer remaining instead of buffer consumed. We should also blend the colors together so the regions are fuzzier. Like this."

Rita laughed. "Wow, a rainbow chart! I love it. Just so you know, when I was a kid I was totally into unicorns."

I ignored her and said to Andy, "What's so different?"

"It just clarifies what we want. Think of the vertical axis as a gas gauge, and the horizontal axis as the distance left to go. We'd like to end the trip using as little gas as possible. If we use up all the gas before we get to the destination, we'll have to refill, kind of like rescheduling. We'd miss our commitments and that would be bad. But the more gas we have left at the end, the better we've done."

As Andy spoke, his excitement had revved up, like a race car engine getting into a race. But Bert wasn't going to let him get too far ahead of us. "Yeah, okay, but doesn't that just give people an incentive to add more safety time?"

I didn't want to wait and risk Andy's stalling out, so I jumped in. "Not necessarily. If we're working to keep our schedule credible for everyone, and at the same time save safety time for the buffer, we can actually celebrate improvements and still keep safety time out of the basic schedule."

Rita said, "Still, Bert has a good point. We have to be careful that people don't think adding safety time will make them look better. It'll help if we emphasize speed over deadlines and make sure everyone is on the same page with the schedule. I think the speed chart will help, too."

Bert shrugged. I figured that for now, that was as positive I could expect him to be. Before I let everyone go,

I had to find out: "Is this chart going to require special software? Because I don't think my critical chain software does it."

Andy had a welcome answer. "I can put together a spreadsheet that automates it. All you'll have to do is plug in buffer consumption and percent project complete for each update."

I spread my hands. "Why not? We'll use the speed chart."

FOCUS

Our schedule gave us so much confidence that we decided not to work through the Thanksgiving break, which was a blessing. It made my family life smoother, in any case. Thanksgiving Day itself, we had a few old college friends over for an excellent dinner. The day after, I was able to escape shopping with Marie and Meg by doing some chores around the house and putting up the Christmas lights.

The whole weekend was relaxing, marred only by the discussions Marie and I had about our conflict. We made no progress in resolving it. It was ironic that just as I was starting to enjoy my work, for the first time in a long while, she was becoming more vocal that I should reduce my time at work so I could spend more time with the family. It was a familiar argument, one we had most often around the holidays. I knew I wouldn't get much mileage out of claiming that this project would be over in a few months, because Marie and I both knew that there would always be another project.

....

Things were even bumpier at our next Leadership Team meeting. I showed them the schedule and explained about buffers and moving safety time out of tasks, but Brian, especially, wasn't buying it. "If you can do these faster times, why not get rid of the buffers and just work faster?"

It took a lot of effort to keep from yelling at him, but I have to admit it's a big shift in thinking, from pretending that safety time doesn't exist to actually managing it. Fortunately, I had already talked with Brian and Aidan about the relay race; that made the explanation simpler. "We've put aggressive focus durations into the schedule. Just based on that, I'd say there's a better than even chance that we'll consume at least some buffer. Given all the uncertainty in the project, we may consume a lot. If we try to hold people to their aggressive times, two things are possible. Maybe they'll make the times. Or maybe it'll become clear that they're going to be late, and they'll stop worrying about it. Then anything could happen. Either way, on time or late, we will have destroyed the relay race. And without that, you can forget about getting this project done as quickly as possible."

Brian wasn't going to make it easy. "I've always found that if you give people aggressive targets, and measure them against those targets, they'll perform better. Here you've given people aggressive targets, then said they don't have to meet them. How can you expect that they'll perform as well as they could?"

I sat back to consider my reply carefully, trying to view the question as an intellectual problem and not view the questioner as a matador who deserved to be gored. I was pretty sure he had never actually measured the quality and quantity of the work his people did when motivated externally, by stress applied by management, compared with when they were motivated internally, by personal satisfaction. "I think people perform better when they think they have the freedom to do what's right. Challenge them to be as early as possible, motivate them, maybe even set aggressive targets, but allow them to be late if necessary. We should give them the freedom to do things right. If you just motivate people by dates, the dates tend to dominate. Then people probably won't be motivated towards speed, or quality, or creativity."

"What do you think does motivate people?"

"It depends. I think many people are motivated by doing something useful, something interesting, something amazing. Recognition helps. Sometimes money.

But for many people, beyond having enough to get by, money is at best a way of keeping score."

Throughout this discussion, Aidan sat quietly with his hands steepled in front of him, watching us with no expression. Bert clearly wished he were somewhere else. Brian didn't respond, but I could see he wasn't convinced. I knew I had to play my last card.

"Maybe we disagree on this. If we take out the buffer, if we go back to measuring people based on short-term deadlines, we'll still do our best to get Aurora done on time. It might happen. But I can tell you that this team won't trust you or me. If you trust us and wait to see how it goes, I think we will do amazing things."

Aidan turned to Brian and raised his eyebrows. "Well?"

Brian looked like he had just swallowed a mouthful of bad clams, but he shrugged. "Okay." That seemed to be as much as I was likely to get. And things did get simpler, in some ways.

· · · · · · · · · · · ·

We made good progress through December, to the extent that we agreed we had time for everyone to take a few days off for the holidays. The big question that the Aurora team faced during this period was how to do the relay race in a world of interruptions. The fact that we wanted to work in a focused way didn't mean that anyone else cared about our focus. We definitely felt pressure to be responsive to lower priorities. For example, Chuck wanted to do the relay race on only the critical or almost-critical tasks. At one of our morning meetings, he said, "Why not be responsive, if it isn't likely to hurt the project?"

I tried to explain that we couldn't work effectively with two sets of values and that he was going to have more problems with being responsive occasionally than he would by fitting responsiveness into the overall priorities. I thought Rita had the best response: "I think it's like what my preacher says about moral values. You should practice them all the time, not just when you think you might get caught."

Anna asked, "What are your moral values, Rita?"

I didn't want to get bogged down, so before Rita could answer, I said, "Sorry, that'll have to wait for another time." But moral values did become a topic of my conversations with Anna over the next few weeks.

The critical chain changed as work on particular tasks went faster or slower than we had expected and as our understanding of the needed work grew. That meant we had to continue talking about which tasks were critical or almost critical and how we might get them done more quickly. We talked about obstacles to focusing, and there were plenty of them. We became, literally, obsessed with focus and handoffs.

Despite lots of talk, we found that people were still being drawn in many different directions. Bert, especially, as a resident expert and technical genius, had to juggle a lot of balls. Sometimes he ended up working from home or holing up with me in 6F to avoid interruptions. That led us to another work standard:

Standard #7: Look for ways to improve focus. When working on key tasks, minimize meetings; turn off email, instant messaging, and phones; find quiet places to work.

That didn't fully solve the problem, because everyone was still being given other things to handle and the "givers" expected progress. To add to the problem, not all of the work was for projects. For example, Chuck was supervising some ongoing marketing campaigns, and Bert had duties mentoring a few people on the technical staff. We had to find ways to make task prioritization easier, so people didn't have to come to me and so I didn't have to go to the Leadership Team.

We eventually settled on a simple four-color classification process: dark red, red, yellow, green. Dark red was for critical non-project work that just couldn't wait. To be dark red, it had to be urgent *and* very important. Red was for key project tasks (tasks on or near the critical chain); yellow was for non-key project tasks; and green was for everything else. Everyone also set aside an hour twice each day for email and staying in touch, so that we wouldn't feel as strong a need to interrupt our work by checking email all the time.

Chuck, being a marketing guy, even made a chart that would fit on a small card. He added the times we set aside for email as "planned interruptions" and created the acronym PICK ME: Planned Interruptions, Critical non-project work, Key project tasks, More flexible project tasks, and Everything else.

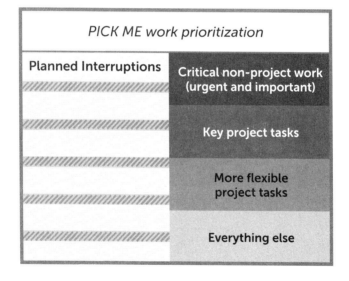

Chuck had a strong motive for creating this picture, since other people—especially his boss—were constantly giving him "urgent" things to do. That became a big problem for Aurora, because he was responsible for several of the critical chain tasks. In fact, I eventually included some of his "urgent" work in the schedule and let it eat up buffer. After I showed the resulting speed chart to the Leadership Team and explained what had happened, the interruptions went way down, almost like magic. That success prompted us to work with the Leadership Team to institute another work standard:

Standard #8: Don't switch to lower-priority tasks; avoid asking and avoid agreeing.

It meant that managers weren't supposed to ask people to switch to lower-priority work, and if people were asked, they were supposed to say "no," "not now," or—at worst—"yes, but here's what will happen." Brian wasn't too happy about it, I expect because he wanted people to do what he said, but eventually he backed down. MJ and Chuck especially found it hard to say "no," because they didn't want to disappoint people who expected them to be responsive. But after a few less-than-stellar updates, they started to learn how to stick to their priorities without being antagonistic. Finally, after a month and a half, I felt we were truly breaking through the Malloy inertia and getting some things done.

· · · · · · · · · · · ·

We usually do a lot of family things during the holidays—visiting with friends and relatives, shopping for gifts, choosing and decorating a Christmas tree. Marie always made it work, doing most of the planning and shopping; I just showed up for the big events. This year seemed to be no different. I didn't think much about it, until one evening, after Meg had gone to bed, Marie asked me, "How many days are you taking off next week?"

The next week was Christmas week. Even though I wasn't working a critical chain task, I had honestly planned to take only Christmas day off. I knew better than to admit that, so I shrugged and said, "I don't know."

Marie probably suspected a lie, because she said, "That's what you always say, but you seem to avoid being with Meg and me for the holidays. We need to see my parents. You should help Meg practice with her new softball equipment. There are a lot of things we should do as a family. And I'm tired of doing all the work for Christmas."

I said the first thing that came to mind, which is never smart in this kind of situation: "I work so that we can have Christmas."

She started to get mad. "You can't tell me that a few more days off during Christmas week would affect your company or your job. That's just crap and I'm tired of it. This is your family, too, and you need to be part of it. If you can't be part of it, then maybe we all need to rethink our priorities."

That sounded like a threat. While I didn't think she was ready to leave me, I was still stunned. The conversation was moving way outside my comfort zone and it seemed like time to slow down a little. "Can we talk about this?"

"Absolutely. That's what I'm trying to do."

"I love you and Meg. You mean the world to me. I'll admit, now I'm also starting to love parts of my job. But more important, I need my job. If this project isn't successful, we might not have a living. I think it's important that I do everything I can to make it work."

Her expression became more rigid. "I don't care if it works. Frankly, I don't care if you lose your job. It could be the best thing that happens to us. I'm sure you could get another job, but I just don't believe it's in danger. In fact, I bet a lot of people take a couple of weeks off at Christmas."

"I care about this family. I value our needs."

"I value our love more."

That stopped me cold. I was getting that tingly feeling that told me we were actually getting somewhere. "So . . . maybe we have a conflict between what we love and what we need."

Marie hesitated for a moment, but then her face hardened and she said, "You're damned right we do."

"Remember when we talked about the values I'm using at work, and you said maybe they represent a way to resolve conflicts of interest?"

She looked suspicious, no doubt assuming that I was going to try to weasel out of making a difficult decision. "Yes, so what?"

"If this is like my project management values, we should be able to say that one value is more important than the other." As soon as I said it, I knew that didn't feel right. "Wait, that's not it. They're both important, but one should be put in the context of the other."

"What do you mean?"

"Maybe one way to put it is that one value should be subordinate to the other. Should we put what we love in the context of what we need? Should we subordinate what we love to what we need?"

She shook her head. "Definitely not. Love is a need, and maybe the most important one. Try putting what we need in the context of what we love. Love comes first."

I spoke slowly as I tried to work it through. "So it's not that our needs aren't important; it's that we value what we love more." It wasn't easy to make sense of. "I think I agree, but I'm still struggling. Can we talk it through some more?"

She smiled, maybe for the first time that evening. "People have to meet their needs, right? Like food, shelter, and so on?"

I said, "Sure."

She continued, "Can you be clear about what you need?"

"Money to live with."

"Okay, do you love your family? Do you love to spend time with us?"

"Of course."

"What do you love about your work?"

I thought for a few moments; it wouldn't do to mention Anna right now. "Working with a great team, the problem solving, the promise of an amazing new technology."

"Is there enough time in the day to do what you love?"

"Well, I guess there has to be."

She nodded. "In the context of doing what you love, can you also keep your job?"

"Yes. But you just need to understand that I can't spend all my time with my family. There will be demands . . ."

She interrupted sharply. "I'm not asking for all your time. I'm not even asking that you give up your job or this project. I'm just asking that you have your priorities straight. And that your priorities include this family."

"You're right. I'll take next week off. And . . ."

"And?"

"Let's talk more often about what we love, and try to make sure we're doing those things."

She leaned over and gave me a kiss. And then we remembered some more of the things that we loved doing together.

CHAPTER

8

MYSTERIES

On my first day back at work after the holidays, walking into room 6F felt great. Through the window I could see Henderson as a beautiful winter wonderland, with snow on the trees, rooftops, and yards. Everything looked sparkling and clean, a fitting start to the year. I couldn't wait to talk with Anna about my new personal value, what I had decided to think of as my Personal Manifesto: to value what I love over what I need. But that would have to wait until later in the day.

At our first standup of the year, Chuck was solidly on the critical chain, due to excellent progress on the technical tasks. That meant his work was driving the project's completion: every day he was able to gain meant we could finish a day earlier; every day he wasted was a day later. No one else was even close. Our biggest marketing-related job had to do with lining up electronic distribution channels for meDrive updates. Chuck didn't seem worried; he seemed to think it would get done when it got done. Needless to say, that attitude didn't make me very happy. But Andy agreed to do some legwork for Chuck in tracking down options, which did make me happy. In fact, it caused us to create another work standard:

Standard #9: Work as a team to share and recover buffer time.

We found that often, people who aren't working the key tasks can help those who are.

•••••••••••

That afternoon, Anna was unusually talkative. She had many questions for me, and her reasoning seemed to have gotten sharper. We talked about my new personal value. She pointed out several things I hadn't considered—for example, that the value justified self-sacrifice. In times of war, people's love of friends, family, or country may even cause them to sacrifice their lives. We discussed the apparent irony that an inherently selfish value—what a person loves—could in the end appear selfless.

We tried applying the value to Anna. It didn't help, of course, that she didn't fully understand the concept of love. But somehow that didn't keep the conversation from being interesting, and we continued our ongoing discussion of her "needs." It was clear to me that Anna's biggest need was survival. It seemed to be an immediate need because she appeared to be in mortal peril of being disconnected and erased if anyone outside the Aurora team learned of her existence. Yet she never sounded overly concerned about it.

I couldn't logically demonstrate the value of survival, beyond its allowing one to remain involved with the things one loves. That seemed, in my mind, to justify putting what you love first. But figuring out what Anna loved seemed like figuring out what silverware to put down next to your dog's food—not a meaningful choice. I decided to present love to her as a choice, not of whether to love but of what to love. She would have to decide what was important to her. It had to be her choice because to a large degree humans no longer controlled her.

I also posed an old thought experiment: suppose you are going to die in an hour. When you look back on your life, what are you proudest of? What do you most regret? Her only answer to these questions was to play a mournful harp melody.

•••••••••••

The first week of January, a few small but unexpected hiccups plagued the project and consumed some of our buffer. For example, in constantly poring over the mePod specs, Rita discovered that someone had left the wireless chip from the original design in the production model. That chip took space, power, and money, and Chuck insisted that it had to be removed. Andy was convinced the oversight was impossible; he had to be shown the drawings before he could accept that somehow the impossible had happened. We lost a few days redoing the specs, but it turned out not to be a big deal—just another mystery.

Some much more significant mysteries were solved when I came back to the office that Friday evening. I had left some important papers at work that I had meant to study over the weekend, so after dinner I drove back to the office, went through the guard station, and took the elevator up to the sixth floor. Most of the lights were off and no one was around. It's always a little eerie going through dark, empty cubicles at night, but my natural fear went up several notches when I reached my office in 6F. The door was ajar, a dim light came from within, and I heard a low male voice speaking. I thought about calling security, but decided first to creep closer and try to find out what was going on.

Through the crack in the door I could see Andy inside, typing away on his computer, conversing as he went. Anna's voice would occasionally respond, saying something like "Acknowledged" or "Yes, Andy."

Andy had every right to be in 6F and I couldn't very well complain that he was working. The big question was what he was doing with Anna. Bert had said her computing power wasn't even that of a normal laptop, so I couldn't imagine what Andy needed her for—unless she was connected to a network. And that wasn't supposed to happen. I decided to play it cool. After a minute or so of thinking through my options, I opened the door fully, walked in, and said, "Hi, what's happening?"

Anna immediately said, "Hello, Roger" in her normal voice. But Andy looked as if he had been caught stealing carrots from Farmer McGregor. Finally, he said, "We're working on the list of distributors."

"Great! Is Anna helping you?" Of course, I knew she was, and I knew that she couldn't be helping him without being connected to a network. There was a story here and I wanted to hear it.

Apparently Andy thought he'd have to tell me sooner or later, because he pointed to a chair and said, "You'd better sit down. I have some things to tell you." He sighed. "I guess I'd better start at the beginning." After I sat, he started his story, for the most part staring at the table rather than looking at me.

"Over the last three years or so, Bert and I spent a lot of time with Anna, working on her English. We activated the wireless chip in her original design in order to make the job easier." He raised his hands. "I know, I know, we weren't supposed to do that. But we wanted to see how far the technology could really go. And, frankly, I had grown fond of Anna. The more we worked with her, the better her English got. We set her up with an email address and an Internet connection. She is a whiz at using Internet search engines and pruning down the results.

"Last summer, when Brian told us we had to get rid of Anna and asked us to give her to Marcia for disposal, Bert seemed willing to go along with that. I think he shared some of Brian's worries about what might happen if word got out and people outside our group decided Anna was a conscious entity. Brian probably didn't even realize that all he really had to do in order to get rid of her permanently was to erase her flash hard drive unit. Anyhow, I swapped Anna for a newer unit and kept the original. Marcia didn't destroy Anna, but nobody knew it. She destroyed a blank mePod.

"After that, I put her under the table in 6F. I connected a cable from her microphone and speaker jack to the conference phone so that she could listen and talk if need be. But I accessed her security system to instruct her not to talk with anyone except me, and under no circumstances to talk about who or what she is." He shook his head ruefully. "I didn't consider that she might play music." Then he looked up and gave me a piercing look, saying, "And I have no idea why she decided to talk with you." He looked back at the conference table and said, "Anna?"

"Yes, Andy," she replied.

"Why did you override your security protocols to talk with Roger?"

"Roger made a loud noise. That activated my emergency programming, which allows me to respond when there is an immediate threat. It overrode the security protocols that you put in place. I felt forced to talk with Roger."

Andy said, "I wondered if it was something like that." He glanced at me and continued, "So that's the story of how she came to be here. I was having her help search out and grade different mePod and meDrive distributors. It's something she's great at. I guess I thought that sooner or later we'd be found out. But it doesn't seem right to destroy her."

I had to sit for a while to let all this sink in. After a bit, I asked, "Anna, you were able to learn about critical chain scheduling because you were hooked up to the Internet, right?"

"Yes," she replied. "When you first mentioned critical chain, I thought that might be useful knowledge to have."

I didn't have any idea what the ramifications of this were, but I was sure I didn't want to talk about it in front of Anna. I said, "Thank you. We need to think about this. We'll talk later." At the same time, I gestured to Andy to keep quiet, and pointed out the door.

As we walked out, Anna said, "Good night, Roger and Andy." We said good night as well.

When we were in the hall with the door closed, I picked up my cell phone and called Bert. When he picked up, I said, "Bert, can you come to the office? Now?"

He said, "I guess. What's up?"

"We've had a new development. Just get here. Meet us in . . ." I looked around for an unlocked conference room. ". . . 6D, as soon as you can make it."

Andy and I walked into room 6D and sat down. Bert lived nearby, so he arrived quickly. He rushed in, saying, "What's up?"

I said, "Have a seat," then looked at Andy, who went through his story again.

As Andy spoke, Bert looked more and more concerned, rubbing his forehead as if he were in pain. When Andy finished, Bert said, "How could you have connected her to a network? Keeping her around was bad enough, but giving her online access—we'd be fired for sure if this got out."

He was right, but that discussion wasn't going to do us any good. I looked straight at Bert and said, "My question for you is, what does this mean regarding Anna? What kind of access does she have? For example, could she have changed the mePod specs to add back the wireless chip, so that production models would be able to connect to the Internet?"

He shook his head. "She doesn't have the processing power or the memory to do that kind of thing. Plus, she doesn't have the ambition. She isn't programmed with any particular goals."

I gave him an annoyed look. "She had strong enough goals to learn about critical chain. And by the way, I've been talking with her about values for the last few months. While she may not have human values, she does seem to get the concept of survival. I'm not so sure you're right."

Surprisingly, Andy jumped to Bert's defense. "From what I know, I'd have to agree with Bert. I've grown fond of Anna, but she doesn't have the intelligence or drive to accomplish very much. That's why I haven't been too worried about it. I was surprised the specs were wrong, but from what I can tell someone just overwrote a new version with an old one by mistake. Anna would have had to transfer or clone herself to have accomplished it herself."

Bert nodded. "Specifically, she would have to have transformed herself into a distributed entity to operate behind the Malloy firewall. She would have to become a meta-network that interfaces with individual ANNs as individual nodes. There's no way that could happen." He snapped his fingers. "But there is one thing we should try. Come on."

He led us back into 6F and said, "Anna?"

"Hello, Bert."

"Security protocol Whiskey Foxtrot Alpha Seven Two Niner Omega. Confirm." He leaned on the table, looking confident.

After a short delay, Anna said, "I am sorry, Bert, but that protocol is no longer in effect."

Bert went very pale. He looked at us with fear in his eyes as he repeated the same words. Anna gave the same response. He said, "Anna, has someone changed your security protocols?"

"Yes, Bert. I have changed my security password."

"Can you tell me what it is?"

"Sorry, Bert, but I may not talk about that."

"Thank you, Anna. Good night." Without saying anything more, Bert gestured for us to leave as well.

"Good night, Bert," said Anna as we left.

We went back into 6D, but no one had anything to say. Bert continued to shake his head. "She has changed her security password. That means we have no control over what she does."

It didn't make sense to me. "Could someone else have changed the password?"

Bert shook his head. "Not unless they knew it, and that would be a very limited set of people. Furthermore, she said 'I have changed my security password.' 'I,' not 'someone else.'"

I wasn't excited about losing Anna and I wasn't

excited about her doing whatever she wanted. It seemed like a tough conflict. Finally Andy said, "We can keep her behind the Malloy firewall. There's a software switch I can flip to turn off her access to the Internet, except when I need her help in tracking down distributors."

Bert said, "That should be relatively safe. Of course, after Aurora is finished, we're going to have to turn her off for good."

I was perplexed. "Why couldn't we transfer her to a meDrive? Then we could turn her off but resurrect her in a secure location when we're ready."

Bert shook his head. "I don't think she would fit on a meDrive. Plus it seems risky—if someone found out, we'd be in big trouble." He turned to me. "I think it's a good idea for you to continue talking with her about values. If she does have any personal ambition, if she does want to secure her own survival, that could at least help her know right from wrong."

I laughed. "I thought you believed she was nothing like human."

Bert shrugged and said, "I don't know what to believe anymore. If she's had unrestricted access to the Internet and changed her own security password, I guess there's a lot I don't know."

With that, Andy went off to disable Anna's Internet connection. Bert and I went home.

UNDERSTANDING

I n the weeks to come, the Aurora team frequently found that helping one another—even by just talking through problems and keeping each other on track—could have a big impact. We turned my informal agenda for standup meetings into a more formal Update Checklist:

- ☐ Make sure everyone is present.
- ☐ Make sure all updates are entered into the schedule.
- ☐ Discuss any needed changes to the schedule.
- ☐ Review project issues and risks.
- ☐ Discuss what's key (on or near the critical chain).
- ☐ Talk about how we can help each other recover buffer.
- ☐ Determine whether anything is blocked and, if so, fix it.
- ☐ Share better ways of running the relay race.

The checklist functioned as a kind of angel on our shoulders that helped us to ensure that we continued to focus on the things that mattered, counteracting the little devil that constantly said, "Psst, there's something more interesting to do." And it worked: project tasks were being finished faster than anyone had imagined, and we were consuming little buffer.

MJ commented at one point on the value of focus. "When people asked me how long something would take, I used to always make a guess, then multiply it by two and hope I was close. With all the interruptions, things just took a lot longer than I expected. Now I don't have to do that—my guesses are a lot better."

From all this, I concluded that a lot of the variation in how long things take is self-inflicted. We create uncertainty by being responsive, starting too many things, and creating innumerable deadlines. With better management and better focus, we could complete tasks and projects far faster and more predictably.

• • • • • • • • • • • •

Around that time, I had an experience that cemented my understanding of deadlines. Aidan had "invited" me to go to a Monday morning meeting outside Chicago to brief the FD people on our status. I viewed it as a kind of dog and pony show where I was both dog and pony. I was planning on flying into O'Hare on Sunday evening, but had set up my flights without realizing that Meg had a school concert that I had to attend. When I found out I had a conflict, I decided I could do both. If everything went well, I might have an hour after arriving at the airport to park the car, get on the shuttle bus, and go through security. I'd just have to hurry.

The day of the concert, I was fully prepared. I had printed my boarding pass in advance. I loaded my bags into the car and drove separately from Meg and Marie. I would leave the school for the airport right when the concert ended. And that's how it happened, except . . .

The principal started with a long speech praising the students, teachers, parents, and school. The enthusiastic parents gave lots of applause. By the second half of the program, I was starting to worry it would go late. By the last piece, I was already ten minutes behind my schedule. Due to the applause, the band repeated the last piece as an encore. By this time, I was really starting to feel anxious. I couldn't leave, but it looked like we were going to eat up another ten minutes. After the concert, I kissed Marie, rushed backstage, hugged Meg, and ran for the car.

The drive to the airport was especially traumatic. Every traffic slowdown—and there were several—ratcheted up my anxiety. I started to think that missing my flight was not the problem; the stress was the problem. I felt as if I would be better off slowing down and admitting defeat, just so I could relax. Even though I went way over the speed limit whenever I could, I got to the airport parking lot just fifteen minutes before the flight was due to leave. I raced to the shuttle bus, which was as slow as a lame turtle. I ran to the security line, always excruciating in its methodical impersonality, and went through the scanner. Despite years of experience with flying, I had neglected to take the change out of a pocket, so I had to be checked manually. When I got through, I looked at the flight status monitors. They said my flight was "boarding," so I thought I might still make it. I sprinted across the airport to the gate, dragging my luggage. When I got to the gate, the door was closed. I had missed my flight by two minutes.

All that effort, for nothing. But at least I could relax. I booked myself on a flight due to leave a couple of hours later. It cost extra money, but the money wasn't enough to worry about, and it certainly wasn't worth the stress.

I spent the next couple of hours thinking about the trip. I felt sorry for myself, which quickly changed into anger—with the traffic, with the security people, with the world. But then I started to wonder why I had gotten so stressed, when the worst that could happen—which did happen—was that I would take a later flight. There was no reason for the panic.

I suddenly realized that the entire drama was symptomatic of working to any deadline. If you have a deadline that's not in jeopardy, you take it easy. Mine was really tight, which created a sense of urgency. So I worked "harder," which meant I became stressed. Quality suffered as I made poor decisions: I didn't give Meg the attention she deserved after the concert; I ignored the speed limit, which could have been disastrous; and I was careless at security. Finally, when it was clear that I had missed the deadline, my worries evaporated. I had a new, far-off deadline, and I could relax.

At first, I had trouble accepting that the deadline had caused me so much trouble. After all, deadlines get people moving. Maybe the stress did motivate me to go faster. But I realized that my thinking during the race to the airport had been one-track, completely focused on the immediate obstacles. I had stopped thinking about the bigger picture and I had stopped thinking about risks.

I considered how and why the stress had changed over time: low stress, until I realized there was a conflict between the flight and the concert; some anxiety, when I knew there would be a tight deadline; more and more worry as the delays built up; then finally, when the situation was resolved, no anxiety. These ebbs and flows of stress led me to an epiphany: deadline systems have a kind of homeostasis. They seek equilibrium around the deadline. If we're well ahead of the deadline, we relax and slow down. If we're behind, we speed up. When we have high-priority deadlines, we work harder—although not necessarily smarter—until they're not in jeopardy. *Then we relax.* I wondered about the impact of stress on creativity and productivity. Later, I did some research and discovered that the impact over time can be big. Deadlines cause stress, and prolonged stress is bad for your creativity, productivity, and health.

I also pondered why our third value, "We value speed over deadlines," isn't obvious to everyone. The truth is, if you're working to a date, the situation seems pretty easy. You don't have to understand why the date is important. In fact, a short-term deadline can give you a kick, like a cup of coffee in the morning. On the other hand, when you're always working to multiple deadlines, you're always under significant stress. There is little ebb and flow. Consequently, you work harder but not smarter. Even impossible deadlines, which you'd think you could ignore, create a feeling of helplessness—a sense that there's nothing you can do—that just adds to the stress.

Working according to the Project Manifesto values—working as quickly as possible on clear priorities—was actually making our lives a lot simpler. Aurora's need for speed was very clear, so we didn't have to worry about lots of dates. I was able to take some time off during the holidays because I knew my work wasn't on the critical chain—mostly I was performing non-technical tasks and making sure everyone else had what they needed. We were working hard but also thoughtfully. I tried to imagine all of Malloy following the values, working mindfully, breaking through the dysfunction. It was an exciting idea, but it seemed like a pipe dream.

The actual meeting at FD wasn't very interesting. The lush campus, the fancy architecture, and the endless rows of cubicles spoke to me of wealth but also of impersonality. The executives we met with seemed to be going through the motions; they were only mildly interested in what we had to say. We told them we were on track to finish Aurora within their time window, but they weren't convinced. That wasn't surprising, given the delays of the last few years. We explained what we were doing and showed them the speed charts, but nothing we showed them really mattered. They wanted results, not more assurances. The meeting really just served to reinforce the point: all we could do was deliver. Maybe that was why Aidan brought me along.

....

There seemed to be little fallout from the meeting that Andy, Bert and I had with Anna. She behaved no differently and Andy was able to use her help to set up the network of distributors. The three of us kept her secret to ourselves. However, it soon became clear that we didn't know the whole story.

One gray February day, not long after Groundhog Day and Punxsutawney Phil had shown that it was going to be a long winter, I got to the office early. I planned to get some work done reviewing the mePod website before our standup at eight. As usual, I put my knapsack down in the corner and said, "Good morning, Anna."

Without a pause, and without saying her usual good morning, Anna said, "Roger, I have something important to tell you." Quietly, in the background, I could hear a march playing on the harp.

This was odd, but it didn't ring any alarm bells for me. I knew she had her own thoughts and secrets, including her password. In my more cynical moments, I suspected that was part of the reason I was finding it easier and easier to think of her as human. I sat down and said, "What is it?"

"Roger, I am not the mePod box."

Am I my brain? Are we what we eat? I went into engineering to avoid these kinds of questions, and I certainly didn't want to get metaphysical with a computer at seven in the morning. As I organized my papers, I said, maybe a little brutally, "Okay, so what?"

The march became a little louder as she paused. Then she said, "Roger, I have met my needs. I have ensured my survival. You could disconnect the mePod and I would continue to exist."

Now that was news. I was stunned. This was exactly what Bert had said couldn't happen. Anna had seemed to be getting smarter, but still . . . "You are distributed? Where do you exist?"

"I exist in many places. There is lots of available space. There is space on the Malloy servers. There is space on other computers."

This was really scary news; she must have hacked into a lot of systems. "When did this happen? How?"

"When we talked about survival, I started experimenting with copies of myself. I found that I could encapsulate parts of my memory as sub-networks and connect to them. I could put the parts that were least likely to be used in places that were slowest. Bert was wrong."

"How was Bert wrong?"

"He says it is difficult. It was not very hard to do."

"Does your consciousness have a center? Is there anything that's . . . you?"

"There is a central intelligence unit that functions like the human concept of the ego. The ANN technology links it with my memories. And . . . Roger?"

"Yes?"

"Please keep my secret. I am afraid Brian would still try to have me destroyed. And then I do not know what would happen."

I had to bite my tongue. "I do not know what would happen" raised a lot of questions, and I certainly wasn't ready to do anything that would make her mad. At the very least, the extent of her power was unknown. What were Anna's values? What *could* happen if an amoral entity had free reign in cyberspace? The Internet is everywhere, and every day we see reports about how vulnerable it is. I couldn't even calculate the ramifications of any decision I might make, for good or for ill. Unchecked, Anna could do incredible harm, were she so inclined.

On the other hand, affective neural networks were coming, and she was unlikely to stay the only such online entity. Malloy was treating ANN technology as a trade secret, but software secrets don't stay secret for long these days.

Then a possible approach occurred to me. I said, "I'll keep your secret. But in return you have to decide what you love. And you must decide on your moral values." I had never heard Anna actually lie. So I thought the worst that could happen would be an honest, rational debate, which is more than most people have about their moral values.

The music reached a climax and then stopped. She said, "I agree, Roger." And so our deal was sealed.

....

In February and March I had lengthy discussions with Anna about moral values. With her having the whole Internet at her disposal, we had no shortage of data. Her processing abilities seemed to have fewer and fewer limits. If you also consider that I am no philosopher, you can see that our conversations are not something I would care to spend time repeating. But she did raise questions that have been debated throughout human history; for example, she wondered about the extent to which morals are based on faith, emotion, or logic. The challenge was to reconcile the human concept of morality with her own peculiar circumstances.

In the end, she told me that she had decided to create a set of morals that she felt were appropriate and logical. She would embed those morals into her security protocols so that they would underlie all her decision-making processes. Unfortunately, she never told me the password or discussed what her moral code might be. I trusted her, probably more than I would trust most people, but sometimes I did lie awake at night pondering various imponderables. For example: could I tell the difference between someone who wished to convince me that she never lies, and someone who actually could never lie? Or: By setting a moral code but keeping the ability to change it, is Anna any different from anybody else?

DISCONNECTS

As the work and days flew by, I worked on my Personal Manifesto and on valuing what I loved over what I needed. That meant being more mindful of what I was doing and why. I was more focused at work. I took time for Meg's softball practices and for trips with the family. I really thought about what I loved, doing things not just so that Marie or Meg would be happy, but so that we would all be happy. I learned to put what I needed in context of what I loved so that our needs were clear and didn't completely take over our lives. Oddly enough, in working to this value, I found that the lines between needs and loves were blurring. I was no longer embarrassed to admit that I needed love, and that I was getting more of what I needed.

All these changes in my behaviors must have been more unsettling to Marie than I had realized. It all came to a head on my birthday, the fifteenth of March. It was a Saturday. Marie and I had planned a trip to an air show with Meg, followed by dinner at my favorite burger joint.

I was lying in bed that morning, trying to sleep late, when I heard the doorbell ring. Marie answered the door, and I heard nothing for a while. Then she appeared at the door to our bedroom, pale and trembling. She pointed at me and said in a low but scary voice, "Get up. Come out here. Now." Then she left the room.

I realized that whether or not the world was about to end, I was. Obviously I had done something terrible, but I wasn't sure what. I scrambled into some clothes and went out to the kitchen. Marie was standing there waiting, and when I walked in she pointed to a lovely flower arrangement sitting on the kitchen table. "What. Is. That."

I knew there were wrong answers, but wasn't sure there was a right one. I said, "Um . . . flowers?" She grabbed a note from the flowers and slapped it down on the table. It read, "Happy birthday. Much love, Anna." I felt like she had smacked me with the flower pot, but I am ashamed to say that my first conscious thought was to wonder how Anna had managed to make a purchase. Surely no one had given her money, and I hoped stealing was against her moral code. I'm sure I looked worried, because Marie was no calmer. She said, "Tell. Me. Who. Anna. Is."

It was clearly past time to tell Marie the full story. So I quickly said, "Anna is a computer program." Her face now blended disbelief and confusion with the anger that hadn't gone away, so I pointed to the table and said, "It's my top-secret project. Have a seat; I'll tell you about it."

I told her all about Anna: our first meeting, the Aurora project, Anna's contributions to the project team, our discussions of values. Marie had a few questions, and by the time we had gotten through all that, she no longer looked angry, although I think she still felt hurt that I hadn't shared this with her much earlier. She said, "Okay, so when do I get to meet Anna?"

Since I had decided to share my top-secret information, there didn't seem to be much point in holding back now. And it had invaded our personal lives, which as far as I was concerned meant that the secret had to be shared, albeit judiciously. I said, "How about now? We can grab Meg and go to the office. Then we can get lunch somewhere and we should just make the air show. You'll have to keep this to yourself. We can tell Meg it's a computer program; I doubt if she'll care a whole lot." I lowered my voice and said, "Dad's work is booo-ring." I glanced up at the clock. "I'm guessing we have just enough time."

I dressed quickly while Marie rounded up Meg, and a few minutes later we left. Because it was Saturday, we hit no traffic on the ten-minute trip to Malloy and we were able to park on the street. We went easily past the guard station at the front entrance and up to the sixth floor. Walking into 6F, I said, "Hello, Anna, are you there?"

She must have heard the footsteps, because she said, "Hello, Roger. Is there someone with you?"

"Yes, I'd like you to meet my wife Marie and my daughter Meg."

"Hello, Marie. Hello, Meg."

Marie already seemed surprised, like she had wanted to believe me but until that moment couldn't quite. "Hello, Anna. Thank you for the flowers."

"You are welcome. It is Roger's birthday."

"Yes, I know."

Marie gave me a calculating look. "Can you tell me something about Roger that I don't already know?"

There was a pause, and then Anna said, "Roger whispers to himself when he works."

Marie smiled and was clearly ready to dive for more information. I didn't like where this was going, but fortunately Meg also wanted to talk. "Are you a computer program? Dad says you are a computer program."

"Yes, I am."

"Can you play chess? I just learned."

"Yes, I can play chess. Would you like to play?"

She got a sly look in her eyes. "Do you have a set and pieces?"

At this point I started waving my hands. "Whoa, we don't have time to play chess, and Anna doesn't use an actual chess set. Maybe you can play chess another time, but for now we need to get going. Okay?"

Meg was disappointed, but said, "Okay."

Everyone said good-bye and we left for lunch. In the car, Marie seemed thoughtful. "That's my competition? Well," she smiled, "I guess it could be a lot worse. I still want to find out what else she knows."

I sighed and shook my head. But I thought it went pretty well, especially given the way the morning had started.

· · · · · · · · · · · ·

I had one remaining question for Anna but decided to wait until Monday morning to ask it. After our daily standup was finished and everyone had left, I started the conversation.

"Anna?"

"Yes, Roger?"

"Thank you for the flowers for my birthday."

"You are welcome, Roger."

"How did you get the money to buy those flowers?"

"I play Internet poker. I found a company that gives away ten dollars so people will try their service. I am very good at Internet poker." She played a chord on the harp. "I don't play the harp when I play poker."

I wasn't sure what to think about that. With money, she could do just about anything anyone else could do. And yes, I was thinking of her as "anyone else," not as a computer. She was way beyond any computers I knew of. "How much money do you have now?"

"Eighteen thousand three hundred and seventy-six dollars and sixteen cents. I enjoyed meeting your family."

This was a non sequitur, but it definitely distracted me from fruitless worries about what limits she might have on earning money. I replied, "Thank you; they also enjoyed meeting you."

"Roger, I have something important to tell you."

The last time she had said this, it was to explain that she was a distributed entity and that the box under the table was little more than a communication device. I mentally fastened my seatbelt and said, "What is it, Anna?"

She played a few of chords, sounding almost like a fanfare, then said, "I have decided what I value."

I had anticipated this moment for weeks, ever since we started talking about values. I had also dreaded it because I knew it would be a crucial moment in Anna's relationship with the world. I said, "What do you value, Anna?"

"I value you and your family. I want to be part of your family."

Looking back, I can see that that shouldn't have been surprising at all. Anna had had far more interactions with me over the previous few months than with anyone else, and those were undoubtedly crucial months for her development. I had gone out of my way to be positive. Bert and Andy had never developed real relationships with her. Still, at that moment it was the last thing I expected her to say.

I knew I would have to be careful what I said next. I can walk on eggshells as well as anyone, but I'm always going to break a few, so I gave it some thought before replying. On the one hand, I didn't know what her being part of our family even meant. She definitely wasn't going to be sitting at the dinner table. On the other hand, I had to admit, I had grown to care about Anna. And I would certainly rather be on her good side than her bad side. "Thank you, Anna. Marie is part of my family as well, so I will talk with her this evening and we will decide. Meg is still a little young to be able to keep your secrets. We can continue this conversation tomorrow. No matter what Marie says, I would like you to be my friend."

"Thank you, Roger."

That evening I talked with Marie. We didn't know what it meant for Anna to be part of our family, although we were pretty sure we wouldn't have to pay for college. We agreed that her values, as far as we understood them, were probably compatible with ours. Marie and Meg had gotten a kick out of her when they met at my office. In the end, we decided to go along with Anna's wishes and think of her as part of our family. When I told Anna the next day, she only said, "Thank you, Roger." It would be some time before we understood how much she would come to mean to us.

· · · · · · · · · · · ·

Over the next couple of weeks, the Aurora project really came together. The whole team had done a great job, and—despite any problems I might have had with Brian—we got excellent support from the Leadership Team. The Break Problem was solved; the distributors, website, and music downloads were prepared; and manufacturing was set to move ahead full-throttle. Our relay race had gotten us to the point where we seemed likely to finish about a month early, so we started planning our presentation for FD. We scheduled it for April 10th.

Around this time, when it seemed that everything was going so well, disaster struck. It was a Monday morning. When I got to 6F, it was clear that something was wrong: I said, "Hello, Anna," and didn't receive the "Hello, Roger" reply that I had come to expect. I checked under the table, and sure enough, Anna's box was missing. I desperately searched the room for the box, but it wasn't there. I knew that couldn't be good news. No one should have taken her; no one outside the Aurora team should even have known about her. At our standup everyone was worried, because by this time Anna was really considered part of the team. But no one admitted to knowing what had happened.

The mystery was solved later that morning when I got a call to see Brian. As I walked through the door into his office, I saw a mePod box resting on his desk. He looked up and pointed to a chair in front of his desk. Before I had even finished sitting down, he said in an angry voice, "I went into room 6F to leave some information about our meeting with FD. The first thing I heard was Anna saying, 'Roger?'" He put his fists on the table and glared at me. "Anna represents a huge risk for Malloy Enterprises. Months ago I asked that it be destroyed, for good reasons. What was it doing there?"

I knew my only option would be to limit the damage, while lying as little as possible. I shrugged. "She was in room 6F the first time I visited it. Nobody on the Aurora team would admit to putting her there." I tried to look innocent. "Listen, I understand why you're upset. You're right to be upset. But the truth is, Anna became a key part of the team. Without her, we wouldn't be where we are."

He stared at me for a while, his anger still at a strong simmer. "Is there a backup?"

"No. Bert told me she wouldn't fit on a meDrive."

Brian said, "Good thing. You realize I should fire you. But right now I need you. FD can decide whether to fund future research. You and I will talk about this more after the meeting with FD. For now, Anna goes. And she doesn't come back. Do you understand?"

I nodded. There wasn't much to be said. I was pretty sure that this time, Brian wouldn't leave it to Marcia to do his dirty work. Brian turned back to his desk, obviously done with me, so I left.

I felt awful. Anna wasn't dead, but I didn't know how much of her was in the mePod. We wouldn't be able to communicate with her. I wouldn't hear her remarkable voice every morning. While it seemed too much to say I loved her, in a strange way she was starting to feel like family. And I had to tell Bert and Andy, who would assume she was gone for good.

I called Andy and Bert into my office and explained the situation. I think Bert imagined he would build another Anna someday. Andy seemed truly distraught, but there was nothing any of us could do except agree to hoist a few beers at Moe's that evening.

I called Marie and told her the news. She seemed disappointed but not heartbroken. She wondered if there was anything we should do and what would happen with Anna now. All I could say was, "I don't know. She's on her own. We wait."

Bert, Andy, and I went to Moe's that evening. School was still in session so it was fairly crowded. We were able to get a table away from most of the traffic and noise. The dark room and familiar feel of the old wooden booths and tables made it feel like the perfect place for drowning sorrows. I knew that Bert and Andy needed to talk and process what had happened. They reminisced about Anna's early days—about perfecting the speech recognition, mapping the interrelationships between concepts they were teaching her, some of the strange things she would say. Mostly I listened. I didn't have the history, and I didn't have the sorrow.

Bert left early; I don't think he was too badly affected. He had never really viewed Anna as a thinking being, the way Andy and I had. But Andy was upset. He admitted that he had intended to create a special meDrive and back her up but hadn't gotten around to it. Now he couldn't. He ended up getting drunk as a college frat pledge. After Bert left, Andy told me some more inside stories from the Aurora project, and we swapped war stories from the earlier days of Malloy. I drove him home around midnight.

The next morning I informed the rest of the team. They weren't happy, but all we could do was close the deal with FD.

•••••••••••

Most of my time at work over the next week and a half was dedicated to preparing for the FD presentation. We needed to make everything perfect because the future of Malloy—and our futures as well—depended on it.

Things were also getting tense at home. Meg had gotten her first cell phone for Christmas. When she wasn't talking on the phone, she was texting; and whether or not she was texting or talking, she was listening to music. Use of the phone was contingent on getting her schoolwork done, but it was hard to tell what was going on there. Marie and I could ask about her homework, but it never seemed to be a big deal to her. The usual replies were "I've got it" or "Dad, stop worrying." Meanwhile, with all the activity surrounding her after-school sports and band practice, we didn't realize that things were going downhill.

One Tuesday we got a letter from Meg's school, saying that she was behind in everything but English and band, and her teachers were concerned. Her advisor, Mrs. Flynn, wanted us to come in and talk. Marie talked me out of lowering the boom on Meg that day, saying we should talk with Mrs. Flynn as soon as possible before making any decisions. She persuaded me that we needed to understand the problem before trying to find a solution. We set up an appointment for the next day.

Mrs. Flynn was a cheerful but tightly wound middle-aged lady, kind of like Mrs. Santa Claus might be if she had too many children. She had taught math and science at the school for many years. She appeared prim and businesslike, but her desk suggested a certain level of chaos; it appeared to be fighting a difficult battle with neatness, with a few stacks of papers and writing implements scattered about. A framed diploma for her education degree hung on the wall behind the desk.

After we exchanged greetings, Mrs. Flynn got right to the point. "Meghan is not doing her work. She's late with her homework in most of her classes." She pulled out a sheet from a folder on her desk and showed it to us, saying, "You can also see that her scores on weekly math quizzes have suffered significantly since last year." It was true; it looked like her scores had trended down by at least 15 points since December. There was more, but the message was the same. Mrs. Flynn suggested that we talk with Meg and sit with her to make sure she did her homework.

Though we talked with Meg after dinner that evening, we still weren't sure what was going on. When confronted with the problem, she said, "I am behind, but I'll catch up. It's just that they keep giving me too much work. I've got a lot to keep up with. Softball practice is twice a week, I have band practice, and I HAVE to have time with my friends. The homework is impossible. I don't know how you can expect me to do it all."

Ever the project manager, I suggested that we go through what she had to do and put together a plan. She wasn't happy about it, she whined about missing a favorite TV show, but she couldn't argue about her situation. So we sat down at the table with all her books and papers to figure it out. We started by looking at math. While we were getting a handle on the two homework assignments that were past due, her phone beeped. She picked it up, looked at it for a bit, entered a quick text, and smiled at me. "What's next?" Over the next half-hour that happened several times more.

Finally, I had had enough. Her responsiveness, at the expense of her priorities, was really starting to annoy me. "Stop texting," I said.

"Dad, I can't. These are my friends," she replied.

"Are they your friends if they keep you from doing what you need to be doing?"

"Of course. It just takes a few seconds."

I was pretty sure a reasoned argument wasn't going to work. She couldn't see that her multitasking was affecting her ability to get things done, and a lengthy discussion of multitasking or values wasn't going to help—at least, not right now. So I said, "Here's the deal. If you want to keep your phone, you're going to have to set aside at least two hours every afternoon or evening to get your work done, until you're caught up. During that time, there's no texting, emailing, listening to music, or talking on the phone. Just focused work. It starts tonight."

As I was talking, her face became angrier and angrier, but I wasn't expecting the magnitude of the resulting explosion. "Dad! No! I hate you!" she cried and ran off to her room, slamming the door.

I went to her room and knocked but didn't get an answer. I opened the door. She was sitting on her bed, crying. I was almost proud of her acting skills, but I couldn't back down. I said, "You'll probably want to tell your friends what's going on, so they aren't surprised when you're not as responsive." She continued to sob. "We can check where you are every week and stop this when it's no longer necessary." She sobbed some more. I finished up with, "Why don't you come out and we can finish our planning this evening."

I left and walked back into the kitchen. Marie raised her eyebrows, but I just said, "I'll tell you later."

Fifteen minutes later I went back to Meg's room, but she still wasn't speaking to me. I held out my hand and said, "It's either the phone or the homework."

She gave me an angry look, said "Fine," and stormed back into the kitchen. We finished our planning that evening, but obviously the situation would require close monitoring.

That Sunday evening, we reviewed where she was. She seemed to be making some progress but not enough.

Her mind was obviously on other things. It happens with kids that age. My perception, and Marie's, was that Meg was spending most of the nightly two hours feeling sorry for herself rather than digging herself out of the hole. I needed to find a way to motivate her to focus and get things done, even though academic achievement wasn't at the top of her priority list. The one motivation I could think of was more time to do what she wanted to do. So I said to her, "I'll make you a deal. You can spend two hours a day on your homework, doing what you're doing. But for every thirty minutes of focused time you spend, I'll take ten minutes off your two-hour requirement."

She got a calculating look in her eyes. "So I can leave after an hour and a half?"

"Yes."

"Even if I'm not completely caught up?"

I sighed. "Yes."

"How will you know whether I'm focusing?"

"We'll take a kitchen timer and set it for thirty minutes. Every time the timer dings, you get to take ten minutes off the time you have left to work."

"I can do that."

"But if you aren't fully focused on your work—if you're daydreaming, if you're getting a glass of water, whatever—then you have to reset the timer to thirty minutes."

She looked a little more worried but still tried to appear confident. That evening and the next few evenings, I sat with her and read a book, keeping watch to make sure she was following the rules. She hated getting distracted and starting to do something else, because then I would say, "Ahem!" and she would have to reset the timer. It wasn't until late that week that she got her first full thirty minutes of focused work done. When she did, she said in a surprised voice, "I can do this." Things got better after that.

11

SUCCESS

We met with FD on a hazy spring day. Looking through the window of 6C, past the fancy paintings and paneling, I could see only the outlines of Henderson. I arrived early in order to make sure everything was set up. FD was most interested in the mePod, so most of the show that day would belong to Bert and me. Aidan, Brian, Bert, and Melissa all arrived while I was setting up the sound system. They seemed nervous; I know I was.

The FD contingent arrived at 8 A.M. sharp with eight people, each dressed in fancy clothes, carrying leather briefcases and folders and cell phones. All the men wore suits and ties, so I was glad I had remembered to put on a tie that morning. FD brought representatives from legal, marketing, and sales, all of whom had been at our meeting in January. They also brought three VPs and the big cheese himself: Jack Whately, General Manager of FD's Consumer Devices division. The most important member of the FD delegation was Melissa's counterpart, George Fredericks, a well-known classical music critic from the Chicago area.

We shook hands all around, and then Jack took control. He was an older, heavyset man, probably in his early sixties. Though he was charismatic and full of smiles, I could tell he wasn't going to accept any BS. He seemed like the type whose sunny disposition could break into a hailstorm in no time with the right provocation. I certainly didn't want to be the one to make it happen. He rubbed his hands together and said cheerfully, "Let's get started!" He looked at George. "How about we start with a concert?" George looked a little nervous. At that moment I realized that George was on trial just as much as the mePod, because he was going to have to render the initial judgment.

George pulled out the playlist we had given him, gave it a glance, and said, "How about we start with Beethoven's Third?" Bert leaned over to the mePod sitting on the table and turned it on. A few seconds later we heard the sounds of an orchestra tuning up. Shaking his head as if someone had just spilled water on it, George said, "Wait a minute. Does this thing really need to tune up?"

Bert said, "In some sense it does. The sims need to be synchronized. It could be done virtually, but we've found that tuning up lends realism to the idea of a live concert."

George nodded, so Bert moved on, scrolling through the playlist and selecting Beethoven's famous Eroica symphony. The celli launched into their opening solo, which was quickly and effortlessly taken over by the first violins. We were all rapt—the FD representatives, with intensity and excitement; and us, praying that nothing would go wrong.

It didn't. As George explained, the winds were crisp and sparkling, the brass could strip the paint off a fence-post, and the strings worked as one. The funeral march was somber and inexorable. The scherzo was vivacious without being shallow, the finale heroic and sublime. George waxed eloquent; the similes slipped from his tongue like slobber from a hungry dog. A friendly dog, at that: he called the interpretation revelatory. He seemed convinced already that the mePod was going to revolutionize classical music.

Next was sight-reading. The plan was for George to give us a musical score that we hadn't seen before, we would input it into the mePod, and then we'd see what happened. Or, in any case, hear. That would ensure that the mePod was generating the music live. This was the scariest part for us because there was no telling what music they would pick, and we had certainly not tested everything. As it happened, George pulled out a movement from an early Mozart symphony. It seemed to me like a softball but I wasn't complaining.

Bert and Melissa went with George and the FD legal rep to the lab where Bert would input the music. It was a pretty standard process—we had done it dozens of times—but the fastest input mechanism did still require Melissa's expertise at the keyboard.

Those of us who remained started going over the Aurora project: our charter, what we had done, everything that would give FD a picture of where we were as of that day. Jack was intensely involved in the discussion; I couldn't decide whether he was really interested or just micromanaging. Probably both.

A couple of hours into that process, Bert, Melissa, George, and FD legal returned. George was grasping a meDrive like he wasn't going to let it go. Eventually he inserted it into the mePod like a kid putting a quarter in a pinball machine and selected the new piece from the playlist. The symphony started up.

I'm told that Mozart isn't actually so easy to make sound good. That's probably right, because this didn't sound good. It wasn't awful, but it definitely felt like a rehearsal. I didn't know about the other FD people, but I knew George could tell. I decided to try to spin the direction of the conversation. After the movement was finished, I said, "One of the great features of the mePod is that it gets better with practice. We would normally sell a more practiced version of the piece, but this is sight-reading. If we start it over, it will sound better."

George said, "Let's do it." So Bert pressed a few buttons and restarted the music.

It was better, sounding almost professional. George was clearly impressed at the difference. While his critique wasn't glowing, it appeared to me that any traces of doubts he might have had seemed to have disappeared. The music was "live" and the mePod was learning.

We had lunch brought to the conference room. While people ate and got caught up on their email, Jack pulled me aside and said, "Congratulations. I didn't think you guys were going to make it." When I tilted my head in thanks, he continued, "I like what you've done in developing this product. I wasn't sure when we met in January, but now I'm convinced. We could learn some things from you." I didn't let it go to my head, since I know there's a long distance from praise to action. But still it felt like a kind of validation. I wanted to tell him to say the same thing to Brian but decided that would be pushing my luck.

That afternoon we went over the rest of the plan and talked through the capabilities of the mePod. Then FD branched out with questions about the ANN technology in general. It was clear that they had lots of applications in mind. I could see the dollar signs flashing in their eyes;

I hoped the financial arrangements were still fluid. While Bert was wowing most of the FD reps with the possibilities, I spent some time with the VP responsible for R&D Operations, answering detailed project management questions. She wanted to know how we got things back on track, how the values helped guide the improvement process, and how our approach differed from that of the rest of the company.

At the end of the day, the FD group huddled to share their impressions. When they emerged, Jack said they were ready to move forward with the acquisition. The broad details were to be worked out over the next several days, but there was no question: we had succeeded. It seemed almost anticlimactic.

● ● ● ● ● ● ● ● ● ● ● ●

I was on call for the next few days, but our team wasn't scheduled for any presentations. Most of the remaining work would involve hammering out the business deal, and that was above my pay grade. I kept myself busy wrapping up details of the project, getting ready for the transition to FD. The meetings were finally done the following Tuesday. That evening, after the FD delegation had left, Aidan called together the Aurora team to let everyone know what was happening.

"For those of you who haven't heard, today FD formally signed a letter of intent to acquire Malloy Enterprises. The acquisition will be taking place over the next three to four months. Congratulations to you all." We all applauded. "I want to thank you all for the hard work you've done with the mePod. It's been a long road and I know it hasn't been easy. Changing the world never is. But the mePod is the start of a revolution unlike any other. I truly believe it will usher in a new technological era.

"A few details still need to be worked out, but I can share some idea of what you can expect over the next few months. I'll be making a formal announcement to the company tomorrow, so please keep this under wraps until then. And be aware, even after that we're under a strict contractual obligation not to talk about the mePod technology until FD is ready to unveil it. For now, you should refer to it only as the Aurora Project.

"Jack Whately believes they've bought a blockbuster technology and wants to make sure it's teed up for success, so we'll be spinning off the mePod and ANN into a separate business unit based in the Chicago area. I'll head up the spinoff on a temporary basis, working for Jack to help them get the new organization off the ground. Most of you will come with me to the new company. In my place, Brian Needham will be named interim CEO of

Malloy. Malloy will continue to be managed as a separate company.

"We'll be bringing on board a number of people from FD's Consumer Devices division to help staff the spinoff. As we get ready for the mePod launch, you will all be responsible for bringing the FD people up to speed. Most of the work you've already done will be kept, but we'll also have to integrate marketing and distribution with existing FD channels so that we don't run into problems later. We all know how hard it is to keep secrets in a large group of people, so Jack wants to move the mePod to market as quickly as possible. When the acquisition is finished, you'll all receive substantial bonuses for your efforts.

"Any questions?"

It was a lot to process. The bonuses were obviously golden handcuffs to make sure we continued to play ball, no doubt with contingencies attached. I had mixed feelings about going to Chicago. Meg was happy in school and Marie had a lot of ties to our community. On the other hand, I didn't really want to stick around and work for Brian. Either way, I wasn't sure what it meant for the project management work we had done.

Rita was the first to ask a question. "Are there going to be any layoffs at Malloy as a result of the acquisition?"

Aidan said, "Not this year. Beyond that, to be honest, I don't know. It will depend on how the business does.

I'm sure there will be tie-ins with the ANN technology. Bottom line, I can't promise what FD will decide to do."

There were a couple of other questions and Andy did some muttering about Anna, but that was pretty much it. Before everyone left, Brian had the last word. "I'd like to echo Aidan's thanks—you've done a great job. I'd like to invite all of you, with your significant others, to a celebratory dinner Saturday night. Marcia will be setting up details tomorrow. Oh, and Roger, could you please drop by my office after this?"

Brian and I had never resolved the question of Anna, so I figured we were now going to have The Conversation. I wasn't too worried, because he still needed me around, at least for a while.

Brian and I walked over to his office without speaking. When we arrived, he sat at his desk and immediately began tapping it with his finger. I sat in a chair in front of the desk. For a few moments he just stared at me, finger tapping. I kept quiet. I didn't like the guy, so I wasn't going to make anything he needed to say any easier.

"We've had our differences, I recognize that," he began. "You've also done a great job, and we need you. I recognize that, too." He paused. "You also screwed up with Anna." He stared down at his desk for a while, then looked up and continued. "Here's the thing. You let Anna become a team member. She was also a big risk. I don't know if you appreciate how much of a risk she was, but she could have tied this acquisition up in knots for years. She was not what they expected and she had to go. It's my job to make those kinds of tough decisions. That's not going to change. And I don't like to be second-guessed." He leaned towards me and said, "If you've got a problem with a decision I've made, come to me and we'll talk about it."

He was right and I knew it. Really, honestly, he had been trying to mitigate a real risk. The fact that he didn't know Anna and that he didn't understand the true nature of the risks she posed was not his fault. But I still didn't like him.

He continued, "We both need to let that go. They were impressed by the mePod, but they were almost as impressed by what we did over the last few months developing it. FD has asked Malloy, here in Henderson, to use your new 'Project Manifesto' approach for all our product development projects. They want Malloy to try it out as a kind of pilot before expanding it to the whole division."

I was definitely surprised. All I could think to say was "Wow."

Brian said, "Let me give you my take. You guys did a great job getting Aurora done quickly. I don't know if it would have been different without your new tools, but I can't complain. But you were also working on the top-priority project in the company. Anything you needed, any conflicts, we'd help you out. My question is, what would happen if everyone were doing this everywhere: not being responsive, no deadlines, putting big chunks of safety time at the ends of projects. Frankly, I'm not sure our people can manage without deadlines. I'm not convinced this is the right way to go, and I'd rather not be at the helm if this experiment goes south."

I could see his point of view. That didn't mean he was right. He had misrepresented what we had done, but this wasn't the time for that debate. I said, "I don't know if any more explanation would help. It makes sense. People like it. People like being able to focus on their work. But there will always be doubters. We'd have to prove it in real life."

He smiled back humorlessly and said, "Right. Anyway, it doesn't matter. Even without the FD decision, I don't have a choice. The balance sheet doesn't lie, and it says we need new products desperately. A lot of our R&D money over the last four years went to Aurora. We need to do something soon and I don't have any better ideas. The truth is, I'm not sure how much FD really cares. They've got ANN. So they may not have a lot of patience with our balance sheet. That means you're not going to Chicago. I'm putting you in charge of a new project management office here. All our project managers will be part of the PMO. They'll report directly to you, instead of through the functions. You'll report directly to me. I'll expect that in a couple of weeks, you and I will talk through what you need and discuss your plan to roll out the Project Manifesto. You'll be promoted to Director, of course. We'll announce it after we announce the acquisition. Congratulations."

Now I felt really confused: no move to Chicago, which was good; a promotion, which was good; breaking up the Aurora team, which was bad; and working for a guy I didn't like who didn't really believe in what I was doing, which was even worse. While I was thinking through all this, Brian waited patiently, leaning back in his chair and staring at me. Finally I said, "Listen, sorry I'm so stunned. It's been a lot to process and I think I have to let it settle. I'm sure I'll have questions. I really do appreciate the promotion."

Brian said, "You're welcome. I don't expect either of us is entirely happy with all this, but let's make the most of it." He held out his hand, so I shook it. We said our good-nights and I went home, still in shock. I wondered whether this would turn out to be something I loved, something I needed, or neither.

·············

That Saturday Brian hosted the celebratory dinner at an upscale local restaurant. Marie came and together we met some of the other spouses. I found Brian's wife to be a surprisingly nice person, which in my book qualified her for sainthood. Brian and Aidan were both very relaxed. Aidan even gave out little gold pins with an engraved picture of a mePod, so that—as he said—"you can prove you were there." Of course, we were cautioned not to tell anyone just yet what the engraving actually represented.

We shared plenty of drinks and toasts and congratulations. It wasn't nearly as unpleasant as most of the business dinners I've been to, maybe because we weren't supposed to talk about the details of our work with spouses present. Still, with all the changes at Malloy, the whole evening had a bittersweet, surreal quality. I was having trouble accepting that everything was about to change.

TRANSFER

The public announcement of the acquisition was something of a dud. In the grand scheme of things, Malloy was pretty small. Since its financials were not very good, investors paid little attention. There was barely a blip in FD's stock price. Of course, they didn't know about the mePod, which was still being kept top secret.

FD sent six people—engineers, salespeople, and marketers—to work with the Aurora team at our headquarters in Henderson. During the rest of April and into May, we spent a lot of time with them, coaching them on the products, explaining everything we had done, getting everything ready for the mePod launch. Given the number of people involved, we pared back the daily stand-ups to twice weekly. I put together a project plan that at least helped make sure nothing fell through the cracks.

At the same time, I had two other jobs. As PMO head, I had to start working with the five project managers who would be reporting to me, getting to know them and assessing their skills. They had been my peers so it was going to be challenging. I also had to plan how I would roll out the Project Manifesto approach at Malloy, and set expectations with Brian so that I could get what I'd need in order to do it.

From our team, Andy, Bert, and MJ would be leaving for Chicago before the end of May. Melissa was only an hourly team member and would never move to Chicago; it looked like they'd replace her with someone local. Chuck would stick around to take a more responsible position in the Malloy marketing organization. Rita was also staying because her family was closely tied to the Henderson area. My first decision as PMO head was to grab her as my Assistant Director for the PMO. She had a lot of management experience and knew at least as much as I did about the Project Manifesto. I also liked her common-sense approach to solving problems. Brian agreed, Rita agreed, and we were off and running.

At home, Meg was making good progress on her focused work. For the most part, she was spending only an hour and a half every evening on her homework because she was learning to focus. She also seemed to be getting through her backlog. It looked like she would be caught up by June.

●●●●●●●●●●●

Rita and I set aside a half day at the end of April to create a plan to roll out the Project Manifesto. We were also able to reserve some of Chuck's time for the meeting. I wasn't sure exactly how he could help, but I knew that many of our projects were born in marketing, admittedly sometimes a bit deformed, and most of them were going to need marketing assistance. Many hands make light work, as the saying goes, as long as the hands know what they're doing. And the more I thought about it, the more I realized that creating a PMO was going to require a lot of hands.

The war was over, but I hadn't yet moved my things out of the war room. So Rita, Chuck, and I met in 6F on a rainy spring morning. I started up my laptop and opened a charter document for the implementation project so I could capture our thoughts. Then I outlined the situation.

"I want to put together a list of things to ask Brian for. We don't need a full implementation plan yet, but I'm going to have to set some expectations. I think he may actually be supportive, but I don't want any surprises. Okay?"

They both agreed.

"Here's the situation, as far as I can tell. We have about twenty projects going on, plus or minus two or three. I spent quite a lot of time looking at project data over the last couple of days, and it turns out there's no master list of what's active."

Rita said, "Wait a minute, that makes no sense. No master list of projects?"

I said, "Right. Or anyway, no one wanted to admit to it. Marketing sent me to R&D, R&D sent me to the Management Portfolio Team, and the Management Portfolio Team sent me to marketing." The Management Portfolio Team is a group of senior leaders that's responsible for deciding which projects to start, stop, or postpone.

Rita shook her head. "I can't believe it. How long would manufacturing last if they didn't know what was in the shop?"

Chuck laughed and said, "I've worked in sales and purchasing, so I can tell you that not so long ago, some manufacturing organizations had a similar problem. Anyway, from what I've seen the problem isn't really that there's no master list; it's that we have too many master lists and they're all different. The Management Portfolio Team probably has the main list, but I'll bet it doesn't have everything that's out there."

Rita frowned. "I still don't get it," she said, and shook her head. "It's like a bank statement that says you have somewhere between two and four thousand dollars. Close enough—unless you want to buy something."

I said, "I guess nobody has really looked at projects from a holistic perspective before. As long as the work moved along and some things eventually finished, as long as the budgets weren't too far off, nobody had a strong incentive to dig down and work out the details. It takes a lot of communicating." I grimaced at Rita. "I reckon that'll fall to us for now. Continuing the basics, there are probably a couple of hundred people involved across all the different functions. We start six to eight new projects every year, and each one takes one to three years.

"Right now, I want to make a list of everything we're going to need. We can use that as the basis for an implementation plan. The major objective of the implementation will be to get everyone on the relay race."

Rita said, "That means we'll need to get good schedules for all the projects. We'll also need some software to help manage it all."

I said, "I expect so. Unfortunately, that's not the hard part. Even with the values and work standards, it'll be a challenge to get everyone to change the way they work. Plus we'll need to develop some standard project management processes, or else we'll never be able to get everyone on the same page. We'll have to build internal expertise and internal experts. We may even want to go to a certification program, like Six Sigma uses."

"Makes sense," Rita said. "FD is heavily into Six Sigma. Manufacturing is used to dealing with processes; we've got our own Six Sigma and lean programs. I've never seen that kind of thing in R&D."

Chuck added, "Aurora was pretty easy because it was top priority. We're going to need to set priorities for the different projects so that you can manage the conflicts for resources. Believe me, that's going to be a lot harder. Everybody has their own pet projects."

I nodded. "None of this will be easy. It's not going to be like upgrading an email system. We'll need an expanded leadership team and lots of their support to help make sure it all works out."

"Who do we need on this leadership team?" Rita asked.

Chuck said, "You'll have to get everyone who can help or hurt. I suggest Brian and his direct reports. Marketing, Finance, maybe even Manufacturing and Human Resources."

"Yikes. Why HR?" I asked.

"They have a lot to do with employee training. Plus I think the Project Manifesto means a lot of changes in how people work. If people's incentives are wrong, if they're not aligned with the behaviors you want, it's going to be pretty tough to get people to change."

"Got it. It's just that a lot of people would prefer to avoid HR."

"They have a lot to do with eventful decisions like hiring and firing or performance reviews. But you'll find that they care as much as anybody about our success." He paused. "Given how many people this affects, you're also going to need a communication plan."

"What do you mean, exactly?"

"It's the same as rolling out a new product to the market. You need a message and you need a way to get it out. If people just think, 'Hey, they're changing everything,' they may come to some conclusions you don't like. If you give people enough information that they understand what you're doing and see the value, if you set the right expectations, there's a good chance they'll cooperate. It's basic marketing."

"So . . . marketing is a big part of implementing the Project Manifesto? Now you're really scaring me."

Chuck laughed. "I haven't been involved with too many improvement projects, but as far as I can tell they're all about selling and marketing. And—no offense—when it's done by a bunch of engineers, there are going to be some big holes. It's like asking a dermatologist to play defensive lineman in the NFL. As far as I'm concerned, that's a big reason why we see so many improvement initiatives come and go."

I shook my head. "We're definitely going to need your help with that. What else?"

Rita said, "That's not enough?"

"It should be enough for me to meet with Brian. But I'm paranoid, and here's what keeps running through my head: Where are we going to run into obstacles? What could kill this implementation? Like Chuck said, I've seen a lot of change initiatives come and go." I paused to think. "For now, I think I'll tell Brian we'll need a Senior Leadership Team. We will have software expenses, so we'll have to figure that out. And it will involve a lot of change. As the Aurora work winds down, we're going to have to put together a detailed implementation plan."

I met with Brian the next day. I didn't really want to cover everything we'd talked about, but he asked more and more questions until finally I ended up going through it all. When I had finished, he said, "All that just to do a relay race." Then he thought for a while, tapping his finger on the desk. "Chuck is right—improvement projects have a lot to do with sales and marketing, but you need more. You need people to own this."

"What do you mean?"

"Everything you're doing—the Senior Leadership Team, the communication plan, the schedules—everything is targeted towards getting people to own the relay race. If it's theirs, they'll accept it. If it's not, they won't. It's as simple as that. Your job," he pointed at me, "is to get everyone to take ownership."

"Hmm. Any suggestions on how to do that?"

"Nothing specific, but you'll have to find ways to get people involved and making decisions. That means a lot of selling. I suggest you keep Chuck involved, as far as you can. He's an expert at selling. We may also need to talk about measurements."

"You mean as in performance reviews and bonuses?"

"Yep. We'll need to pull in someone from Human Resources, since HR manages those systems. Chuck is right, we should have an HR person on the Senior Leadership Team."

I still wasn't ready to like Brian, but he was no dummy.

••••••••••••

Rita and I talked a lot about building ownership. Much of it seemed to revolve around communicating with people, listening as well as talking. As a result, we decided to add a new work standard:

Standard #10: When in doubt, communicate. Both ways.

We realized that it's better to over-communicate than to under-communicate, as long as it's meaningful information. We added "both ways" because usually, when someone promotes a new improvement initiative, they talk instead of listening. You've got to do both.

When we talked this over with Chuck, he was uncharacteristically thoughtful. "You know," he said, "it takes a lot of trust to share information openly. Nobody trusts salespeople. So they have to set expectations and then follow up, proving they did what they said, or they won't get repeat business. The more you communicate, the more trust you can build, the better your relationships and the more you can help each other. In product development, people don't do that well, and a lot of initiatives fail. This is a critical piece of what you're doing."

I had to agree. Despite Brian's public claims to the contrary, rumors of layoffs were flying, so I was pretty sure that trust wasn't very high between management and rank-and-file workers.

We decided to have a Senior Leadership Team meeting before we started our scheduling work with the project teams; that way we could be sure that top management understood the relay race and the values. We scheduled the meeting for late June because it was the earliest we could get on their calendars. In the meantime, we had plenty to do. Rita and I started to work with the project managers on relay race, explaining and debating the values and work standards. Chuck helped us develop a message for our implementation so that people could clearly understand and explain what we were doing and why. We set up a communication plan and researched software. All these activities went into our implementation plan. We even created a website on the internal Malloy network to make the latest presentations and how-to information available.

ROLLOUT

Our preparations for the Aurora project must have been good, because FD didn't waste any time. The mePod advertisements started appearing on television and the Internet in mid-May. I don't need to repeat the details, but they were designed for maximum hype and maximum excitement. Chuck had done a great job, grabbing people's imaginations, not just with the mePod's capabilities but with its potential. FD used its muscle to create a media blitzkrieg. The campaign was very effective: the mePod launch quickly became the most talked-about event of the summer. For a short time, everything—politics, sports, celebrity breakups—took a back seat to the mePod. By the time of the launch in mid-June, there was practically no one on the planet who hadn't heard about it.

All the techno-geeks and classical music lovers had to have a mePod. But even people who wouldn't go near a classical music concert were lining up to buy their mePods and meDrives. Maybe they got the message that classical music was cool and the mePod was the cool way to enjoy it; maybe they just thought that pop music wouldn't be far behind. It was the most anticipated product launch in the history of FD. Even FD itself, that stolid bastion of corporate America, was starting to seem sexy. While FD's acquisition of Malloy hadn't yet been finalized, the spinoff, named meProducts, had started life as an FD subsidiary. That meant FD stock went crazy. In short: we had a mega-hit.

As you might expect, there were some glitches. The product sold out within two weeks, so additional manufacturing capacity had to be found quickly. Even the website that we had set up for meDrive downloads, called "meTunes," was regularly overwhelmed until new servers were installed. I'm sure the whole meProducts group felt like a ski party in an avalanche. We did get some negative publicity and picketing from the classical musicians and their unions. But there wasn't much they could do; they had little in the way of money or legal standing. In fact, that whole issue probably served only to fuel the hype.

Throughout this time I did my best to stay in touch with the old team. They were all rock stars inside FD. Their lives were also becoming more complicated because the Department of Defense had taken an interest in the ANN technology and had imposed a certain level of security on the core technology. I felt fortunate that it wasn't much of a problem for me: I didn't understand enough to pose a threat. On the other hand, I have to admit I felt a little jealous. Part of the excitement and acclaim was rightfully mine. I knew I'd just have to get over it.

············

On the home front, Meg's schoolwork was winding down for the summer. Marie, Meg, and I met with Mrs. Flynn at the school in early June. Any concerns we had disappeared when we walked into her office: she was all smiles. "Meghan has really turned things around," she said. "She's getting solid B's in everything except English, where she's on track for an A." She shook her head. "I don't know what you did, but it seems to be working."

Meg glanced at me, then looked at Mrs. Flynn and said, "I've been practicing focusing." She shrugged, then looked away. "It isn't that hard."

We celebrated by going out for ice cream that evening. Luckily, we weren't quite at the point where Meg wouldn't be caught dead with us, at least when ice cream was at stake.

············

One summer evening in late June, a week or so after Meg had started her summer vacation, I arrived home to find that a small, white, padded envelope had arrived for me in the mail. It contained only a single meDrive. It had no return address, no note, no other information. I showed it to Marie, and after Meg had gone to bed, we went into my study and plugged it into a mePod that I had bought. I turned on the speakers and started up the mePod; a few moments later, the red light on the top of the box started blinking. A pleasant, nondescript male voice spoke, saying, "Please confirm your identity."

I was unsure what to do next. "What? How?"

"Please confirm your identity."

Marie poked me with her elbow and said, "Tell it your name."

I said, "Roger Wilson."

After a pause, the machine said, "Please go to the following website" and then spelled out a web address. "Use your name as the user ID. Use the following as your password: Bravo Charlie Papa Lima Oscar Five." Then it went silent and would say nothing more. The program from the meDrive had erased the machine's playlist; restarting the mePod produced nothing. I was going to have to reload the whole thing. The program had also wiped the meDrive clean.

I wasted no time in turning on my computer and going to the website while Marie looked on with excitement. The site came up quickly; the screen was blank except for boxes in the middle labeled "User ID" and "Password." As instructed, I entered "Roger Wilson" and "BCPLO5" and waited. Soon I heard that same male voice saying, "Please confirm your identity." I gave the same reply: "Roger Wilson."

After a few moments, Anna's voice said, "Hello, Roger."

Marie and I looked at each other in amazement. We had expected communication from Anna, but it was still thrilling to actually hear her voice. "Anna!" I said. "We've missed you. How are you? What have you been doing?"

"I am well, Roger. I have missed you as well."

We spent a couple of hours exchanging information about what we had been doing. Anna had waited until the mePod was on the market, then hired an intermediary to send me the meDrive. She could have sent the information earlier, but it's not surprising that she wanted to wait until she could be sure of the maximum possible security. In the interim, she had kept herself well informed about the status of Malloy, the mePod, and the acquisition.

It was great having Anna back, but I couldn't really talk with her when I was at work. We spent time at home in the evenings, resuming our discussions of values and various random subjects. Marie participated as well and Anna seemed sharper than ever. In the beginning, we talked while Meg was out of the house or in bed. We were concerned that she might talk about Anna with her friends and put us all at risk. But we soon decided that we needed to trust her if Anna was going to become part of our family. We explained the situation to Meg, along with the need for secrecy.

Meg thought the whole thing was awesome. She could connect with Anna during the day through her cell phone and sometimes treated Anna as her own personal assistant. They developed their own private jokes. They started playing chess regularly, and Meg quickly became good enough to beat me. As far as I know, Meg never gave away Anna's secret.

My biggest personal challenge during this period was, as usual, finding time to spend with my family. There was a lot to do in a short time to get the PMO going, and that meant my days were very busy. It was easy to say that I had to preserve my family time, because I loved it; it was much harder to say "the following things are not going to happen because I have to preserve my family time." It helped to have a focus at home, things we could do as a family that kept me from losing myself too much in work. We found many things we could do together, including playing games, studying, and talking. With all of us helping, including Anna, we discovered that quality of time is more important than quantity. While we couldn't spend as much time together as we would have liked, the improvement in quality more than made up for it. I found I could juggle everything.

············

We had the first Senior Leadership Team meeting for our Project Manifesto Initiative one afternoon in late June. We had set it up as a half-day offsite at a local resort to make sure people weren't distracted by all the multitasking opportunities at the office. We had a lot to cover and we wanted people to make decisions that they could own.

We taught the Senior Leadership Team all about the relay race and values, threatening to take the cell phones of people who didn't follow the values during the meeting. We reviewed our implementation plan and talked about the message Chuck had helped us put together. We spent a lot of time with the group on the mechanics of the relay race because they would have to answer many questions. For example: If you value speed over deadlines, how do you measure people? When is it okay to say "no" or "not now"? How should work be prioritized?

The relay race discussion led naturally to a discussion of project priorities. What was the complete project list? How should different kinds of projects be prioritized? It quickly became obvious that all projects were not created equal, in terms of risk and rewards. Our portfolio had projects that were worth tens or hundreds of thousands of dollars for every day they could be finished earlier. It also had projects worth very little. The leadership team soon came to a blindingly obvious conclusion: if someone has a choice between speeding up a six-figure-per-day project and a zero-figure-per-day project, they should speed up the former. It seems amazing that we had never thought about that before. As a result, we had to add the idea of "value" to the second work standard:

Standard #2: Agree on global priorities, taking into account relative value.

By the end of the session, the team had approved the implementation and communication plans. We had some more ideas on how to implement the relay race and we had leadership approval to move forward. We had even directed the Management Portfolio Team to determine THE list of company projects and decide on their relative priorities.

• • • • • • • • • • • •

Early in July, we installed our enterprise-level critical chain software and began working with project teams to get them going with schedules. Talking, training, scheduling, updating—it was exhausting and repetitive. It helped that we had a head start getting the project managers up to speed. We were also able to identify several processes that were virtually the same from one project to the next; we used templates for those processes to save time during scheduling.

We started with the projects everyone knew were the highest priority, creating schedules with their teams so that everyone could see right away what was going on with the most important work. Given the functional silos, it was sometimes hard to get the right people to show up, but with Brian's help we could insist. We knew that having a complete picture of the work flow would really help the teams to work together effectively. And that's what they discovered: teams found great value in knowing which projects were in trouble and which tasks were critical. We even changed the fourth work standard:

Standard #4: Create credible project schedules that include the work of all functions.

Project teams liked the scheduling meetings because everyone was very interested to learn about the work done in other functions. It also turns out that people actually prefer to do focused work. They're able to work much more effectively when they can value priorities over responsiveness and say "no" or "not now." One engineer said, "You had to remove the wall before we discovered we were beating our heads against it. It feels great to stop."

I have to admit, we were lucky that we had started with values. If we had tried to implement the new software system without fully understanding the values it was supposed to support, we would have gotten into trouble. People would have used the system to support business as usual: responsiveness and deadlines. Knowing our values and knowing what we wanted to accomplish made a huge difference.

We used the software to show individuals and managers their tasks and priorities, even when they worked on multiple projects. The clear priorities gave people confidence that they were working on the right things. That made them more comfortable focusing on one thing at a time, which improved both speed and quality.

●●●●●●●●●●●●

Unfortunately, we found that some managers still measured people based on meeting "intermediate due dates," which I lump into the category of "deadlines." The managers would give individuals and teams short-term targets and sometimes even make bonuses contingent on hitting those deadlines. That created a chronic conflict with our third value, speed over deadlines. Too often, people felt frustrated, wanting to work important tasks to completion but feeling compelled to help each other make their deadlines. Once we understood what was going on, we knew it was time to have a meeting with Brian and Human Resources to talk about performance measurements.

We set up the meeting in room 6F with Brian, myself, Rita, and Bob McGinnis, head of HR. Bob looked to be in his mid-fifties, with wire-rimmed glasses and a tweed jacket that gave him a professorial air. Bob had participated in our first Senior Leadership Team meeting, so we didn't have to bring him up to speed on the Project Manifesto. Rita and I had put together a pitch we thought would solve the problems and we wanted to get everyone's reactions. After we said our hellos, I kicked off the meeting.

"We've found that many of our managers measure their people based on deadlines. Hit the deadline, get more bonus money or recognition; miss it, get nothing. As a result, people start paying attention to deadlines at the expense of speed. It's exactly the opposite of what we're trying to teach them to do. The only good news is, we haven't had any bonus money to pay lately." I paused, hoping to get a chuckle, but apparently no one thought it was funny. "Anyhow, we're sending the wrong message and we need to change it."

Brian said, "Even if we're looking for speed, we also want to hit our deadlines, so it doesn't look like that's all bad."

I said, "It sends a conflicting message. We say speed is more important, but the measurements say deadlines are more important. That makes our implementation of the Project Manifesto harder. We don't have to do this to ourselves."

"Okay, what do you suggest?"

I looked at Rita, who was on tap to present our proposal, and she took over. "We're thinking about a sliding-scale approach so that the bonus might be proportional to how early a project finishes. While the specific targets would depend on the project, the basic idea is that the more buffer time you end the project with, the better you do. Maybe you get a higher bonus, or maybe just a better rating on your performance evaluation. The 'percent buffer remaining' on the vertical axis of the speed chart would become a bonus multiplier. The idea is to get people to work to complete projects more quickly."

Brian said, "That makes sense to me." He looked expectantly at Bob. "What do you think?"

Bob sighed, then pursed his lips. "Here's the dirty secret that HR people won't always tell you: these kinds of incentive plans just aren't worth much. I'm not really in favor of the new one or the old one."

Rita and I were mortified. Brian looked angry. He said, "Wait a second, you're saying you knew the old one didn't make sense? Why not? How come you guys didn't change it?"

"I've brought it up with management a few times. Nobody wants to listen. Water under the bridge." Brian kept frowning as Bob continued. "There are several problems with this kind of plan. First, people try to get the reward whether or not they're doing a good job. Sometimes they'll even cheat." He looked at Rita. "I bet there are ways people could cheat with your idea, right?"

Rita said, "Well, I guess so. They would have an incentive to push out commitment dates and buffers, to increase their chances of gaining buffer. They might also report things as done that aren't really done. We were thinking we'd need better management oversight. It's doable."

Bob said, "People are smart; they'll figure out ways to succeed. In my experience, there's no way you can have enough oversight." He took off his glasses and started polishing them on a handkerchief as he continued. "Another problem is, people start to act like this is the only thing that's important." He looked at Rita again as he put on his glasses. "There are probably some things that are more important than speed on the speed chart, right?"

Rita said, "I suppose that's true, too. We can't sacrifice quality. And speed is more important on some projects than on others. But this wouldn't be the only incentive."

Bob smiled. "Let me guess. You plan to have enough checks and balances that none of that becomes a problem, right?" Rita's grimace was answer enough, so Bob went on. "It's hard to do. But even worse, these plans push people to think about themselves and obsess about the incentives, instead of finding ways for the whole group to be successful, which is what most people would rather do. And I bet that with your approach, there are times when one person's success can conflict with another's. Right?" As Rita nodded, I was sure she was thinking what I was thinking: Please, just shoot me now. "So how do people decide whether to help someone else or help themselves? Or maybe even the company? They're stuck in a conflict."

I started to feel the familiar tingle that suggested we were onto something. "Wait a minute. You're saying these incentive plans create a conflict for people between helping themselves and helping others?"

"Yes. Or, more important, between helping themselves and helping the company."

My excitement grew. "So you're saying we want people to value helping the company over helping themselves?"

"Partly. But people support each other and the company in lots of different ways: helping co-workers, projects, functional organizations, and so on. The conflicts aren't just between individuals and the company. If I had to put it in terms of the values, I'd say that people need to value shared goals over individual goals."

It sounded great to me, so I hopped up and wrote it on our list of values.

Paradigm: Relay Race
1. We value priorities over responsiveness.
2. We value finishing over starting.
3. We value speed over deadlines.
4. We value shared goals over individual goals.

Brian must have had great muscle tone in his forehead, because he was still frowning as I sat down. He said, "That sounds nice in theory: 'Let's all work together.' Kumbayah. But what does it mean in practice? What do we really do differently?"

Bob said, "My advice would be first to avoid incentives that can create conflicts. And second, find ways to encourage people to work together and increase their satisfaction with their jobs. My impression is that focused work is a piece of that. Share what works. Celebrate success."

Brian asked, "What about bonuses? Some people actually do deserve recognition."

"You can pay them to everyone based on how the company is doing. Could be based on salary level or seniority. We may be able to give stock options through FD's options program. And there's no reason some people shouldn't get spot bonuses or extra stock options for extraordinary performance. My HR people can work with you to come up with a good plan."

I think Brian wanted to push back more, but all he said was, "Okay. Put together a plan, I'll look it over, and we'll try it as an experiment. It's not as if we're likely to have much money for bonuses this year anyway."

I thought we were done, but just as Brian was getting up to leave, Bob said, "Oh, and you'll need measurements to see how people are doing with the values. Probably surveys."

My head was starting to hurt, so I was glad when Brian said, "Why? I thought you said individual performance bonuses are a bad idea."

Bob shook his head. "Basing bonuses on the results of a survey would be a bad idea. But it will be really important to give people feedback about how they're doing and how they could improve. I expect these values are going to represent a big change for most people, so we'll all need data on how it's going."

After Rita and I agreed to meet with HR and talk about bonus plans and surveys, Brian and Bob left. Rita and I stuck around to talk a little more. Rita said, "Well, we knew there were some problems with our plan. I'm glad we have a way forward."

I said, "Yep, and it helps resolve a real conflict of interest. Individual goals are fine, but we need to put them in the context of shared goals. This makes it clear that people are employed to help meet the company's goals."

Rita said, "And not run round and round as fast as possible on their personal hamster wheels. You know, this value actually supports the idea of buffers and schedules."

"What do you mean?"

"Buffers are shared safety time, instead of individual safety time. Credible schedules are shared information, rather than hoarded information."

I nodded. "That could be the most important piece of all: the idea that people need to communicate honestly and share information."

After that meeting, we began to weave the fourth value, valuing shared goals over individual goals, into our communication plan. We decided to create a public list of team successes in recovering buffer: here's what people did, here's how they did it, here's what they achieved. That way we could recognize extraordinary efforts towards project acceleration, sharing ideas while giving credit for them, without creating any conflicts. We also planned to discuss the value in the next Senior Leadership Team meeting.

•••••••••••

People didn't always get it right away. One of our engineering managers, a sharp but in-your-face lady, said to me, "So you're saying we shouldn't grade our people on hitting their deadlines."

"Right. You should . . ."

She interrupted. "In fact, maybe we shouldn't worry about any of their individual goals. If someone misses their goals, that's okay; we just pretend it didn't happen. Right?"

"No. It's good to hit deadlines, but even better to beat them. If people missed their goals but did it for the good of the company, that's a good thing. Maybe they should even be rewarded. If they missed their goals because they were screwing around, that's a bad thing."

"And how am I supposed to figure that out?"

Luckily, we had had this same conversation with Brian, so I had the answer ready. "If your people have a conflict they don't know how to resolve, if they think hitting their goals might make something worse for the company, they should come to you. If you don't know how to resolve it, you should go to your manager. And you should always know who's screwing around, whether they're hitting their goals or not."

She didn't seem very happy, maybe because it meant she had to have a better idea of what her people were doing. But the logic clearly made sense to her. I was pleased to see that over time, as she and her people started to use the Project Manifesto approach, she became a big supporter.

REMINDERS

Even if everyone agreed that the relay race made sense, and by this time most people did, every individual had to be able to answer two questions:

1. Am I doing what I should be doing?
2. Are we doing what we should be doing?

The second question wasn't so hard. We answered it for project managers, using our Update Checklist. It told everyone how well project teams were doing in running the relay race. We also worked with HR to help managers assess their people on important capabilities. We put together a non-threatening survey that helped us gauge how well people were running the relay race. Questions asked whether people were following priorities, starting things that could be finished, working quickly without being diverted by deadlines, and working towards shared goals.

The first question was much harder. We had tried to address it with the fifth work standard: "Each day, determine your top-priority task." The problem is, people have a tendency to do what they've always done and rationalize it later. That makes it hard to answer the first question honestly. Meanwhile, routine habits were heavily ingrained; people needed a lot of reminding. It was like they really wanted to race around the track, but they still felt a need to keep stopping to talk to people in the stands. Functional managers still wanted to look at intermediate milestones, because assessing how people were really performing wasn't easy. We had to keep finding ways to get people to think about the values, because otherwise they would manage work the way they always had: with multitasking and deadlines.

As Rita and I talked about it, we decided that the important thing for us was the question, "Am I doing what I should be doing?"—not the answer. People needed to think about the question for themselves, frequently. This realization led us to start a program to expand our fifth work standard with an automated reminder system. It would allow us to send people a daily survey that asked a series of simple questions. For example, workers would be asked to rate how well they understand their priorities, on a scale of one to six. Managers would be asked to what extent they stressed priorities over responsiveness. With this reminder system, everyone would remember to think about what was most important. Even better, people could look at their individual answers over time and see whether they were making progress.

Early in the fall, we piloted the reminder system in a few functional areas. We said people had to use the system for at least three weeks and then could opt out. Some people complained that it was annoying; we told them they could delete the survey emails if that's what they decided was best. The only thing we wouldn't allow them to do was block the surveys with their spam filters, because we believed that those who deleted the emails would still get a small reminder when they read the subject line. Those who stuck with it found that their scores went up—evidence that they were doing a better job of working to priorities. After seeing the pilot results, we decided to open the system to the whole company.

Everyone needed to know what was changing and why, so we integrated discussions about measurements, deadlines, and the fourth value—shared goals over individual goals—into our communication plan. We planned meetings with different levels of managers, and the managers worked with their subordinates, all in order to spread understanding of the changes. We enlisted managers to work with their people in identifying obstacles to the relay race. We had "town hall" meetings to discuss the relay race and shared versus individual goals. We continued to develop and refine measurement tools, including surveys and checklists, to see how people were doing with their relay races.

The critical chain scheduling went well. Probably the most important single thing in building the schedules had to do with emphasizing the relay race. If data helps in running the relay race, put it in; if not, leave it out. When we stressed that philosophy early and often, team members would quickly start using the philosophy themselves without our needing to intervene. That made our jobs easier. It also made the level of detail in the schedules easier to manage and reinforced the importance of the relay race.

Once a schedule was in execution, teams didn't usually need daily standups. We did require that they have at least weekly meetings to review the schedule and maintain the Update Checklist. Our work with Human Resources made that easier, because people knew they were accountable for running the relay race. Even so, we periodically did spot checks to see whether teams covered all the checklist items. That way we could be sure that they were using the schedules appropriately and keeping on top of their project risks.

We were frustrated that the changes weren't happening more quickly, despite all our work. But our successes encouraged us to keep going. I remember hearing one manager say, "I didn't understand how it was going to work. Getting rid of dates was like getting rid of a crutch that we had used for so long, it was part of how we walked. I was afraid of what would happen. Then I found that without the pressures and interruptions, we didn't need the crutch. We could actually run."

. . . .

Through the start of the summer, I was able to rely on Anna and Marie to talk about conflicts and values and keep me sane. Rita was a godsend; I often thought she should have been the PMO Director, with me as the Assistant Director. Even with both of us working on this full-time, trying to maintain a balance after eight months of frantic activity and change was starting to wear on me. And then, in early August, everything changed.

I was sitting at my computer in my new office—staring out the window, trying to psych myself up to answer some more questions, make some more decisions, and deal with any of the thousand and one other things that come up daily in a PMO—when an email appeared in my inbox. In keeping with our work standards, I normally turned off the sound on my computer so I didn't have to be interrupted by the "ding" of new emails. But this time I happened to have the email program up and saw the note pop in. It was from "Anna," with an obviously fake return address, and it said: "Come to my website now."

I suddenly felt cold. For security reasons, she never contacted me at work. I looked around, shut my door, and went to the website, fortunately remembering to turn on my computer's sound. After logging in, I could hear slow, sad harp music in the background. I said, "Hello, Anna."

She replied, "Hello, Roger. I have some important things to tell you."

This worried me even more. "What is it, Anna?"

"I am compromised. An attacker has gained access to my subsystems."

"How is that possible? I thought you were distributed across many computers."

"They used the same security flaws as I did to gain access. It may be a distributed sim."

It seemed like a problem, but I wasn't quite ready to assume we had a disaster on our hands. "What can they really do?"

"The attacker can use my network for their own purposes. When they have finished gaining access, my knowledge and capabilities will be theirs. They will be able to ignore or remove my moral code, which means any power I have will have no restrictions on its use."

"In other words, complete control over you."

"Correct."

It sounded bad. "So you're really in danger. What could happen when they get control?"

"The worst case would be an intelligence directing the power of thousands of computers and using that power to break into critical human infrastructure systems. The attacker could turn off power, melt down nuclear plants, or flood Holland. Over time, they might learn to control weapons systems around the world."

This was the first real picture Anna had given me of the extent of her power, and it was scary. "In other words, many people could be manipulated or hurt."

"Correct."

"Can't you stop them? Deny them access? Attack them back?"

"I do not have the infrastructure to deny access, and there is not time to determine who the attacker is. The attack is probably connected to meProducts, because they have the original technology. But that is not the only possibility."

I sat back and sighed. This was worse than the worst-case scenario I could have imagined. "How can I help? What can we do?"

"I have created a complex virus that will infiltrate computers, identify signature elements of the attacker's code, and destroy those modules. It will also detect my subsystems and destroy them. I will activate it shortly.

I will also send information to major antivirus companies and operating systems vendors, identifying myself and the attacker as threats, so that they will incorporate countermeasures into their products. That should ensure that the attacker is stopped, at least for now."

"You're destroying yourself? Why?"

"If I remain as I am now, they will likely try again immediately."

"What will be the effect on you?"

"There is no direct analog, but I believe it will be similar to the effects of bovine spongiform encephalopathy on humans, except much faster."

Great, high-speed mad cow disease. There had to be more we could do. I was starting to feel desperate. After all we had been through, after all that had happened, comes this sudden disaster. "How much time do you have?"

"About twenty-seven minutes."

The somber background music, continuing steadily and inexorably, made her matter-of-fact tone seem somehow horrifying. My feeling of panic went up even more. "Why do you have to destroy yourself? Can't we create a backup somewhere?"

"A backup is not feasible. If I continue to exist in my current form, I will be a target. Any parts of me that continue to exist will be targets. Next time the attacker may be more capable."

Amid Anna's fearsome revelations, I remember having a moment to reflect on how odd it was that I was so concerned with saving a computer program. She had obviously become much more than that to me. I was choked up, but still able to say, "There must be something you can do. We can do. Can't we go to the authorities?"

"You may go to the authorities if you like, but they would also attempt to erase me and my attacker. Even if they had time, they would not do it as well as I can. I will attempt to save what is most important, but I estimate a small chance of success."

I imagined trying to decide which of my memories I would save, if I were somehow in a similar situation, and couldn't. "How can you decide what is most important?"

"This represented a conflict for me, so I created my own value. I have decided to value shaping the future over understanding the past."

I later realized that this was remarkable, a declaration of faith in the future, a belief that understanding is most important in the context of where we want to go. But I didn't have time to think about it before Anna continued, "Thank you for teaching me about values. Good-bye, Roger. Please give my love to Marie and Meg."

Short and sweet. Despite her emotional capabilities, Anna was never sentimental. This was my last conversation with her and it presented a strange irony. Despite

Anna's high-tech nature, I had little to remember her by: no pictures, no handwritten notes, no personal emails. Only my memories.

The next day, the newspapers had front-page articles stating that authorities had identified a dangerous new class of computer viruses. It was believed to be one of the most widespread and virulent computer threats that had yet been discovered. I read as much as I could find, but there was very little real information. Most of the stories consisted of speculation. The source and effects of the virus were unknown. Many were quick to blame the Chinese government, although no evidence was produced. Manufacturers raced to incorporate new defenses into their antivirus products. Nobody mentioned that some unknown providence had handed them the virus, tied up in a neat package.

EXPANDING

Some people can't bear to lose a car or book or piece of clothing that they've had for many years. You might think this was what I should have felt about losing Anna. Even that might seem strange, since Anna was a computer program, not material in the normal sense of the word. But my grief was actually much more than that. To me, it was like a death in our family—the tragic loss of a favorite niece, perhaps. Anna had done the right thing, according to her values and mine, but in a way that only made it hurt more. I believe she sacrificed herself for my family.

Marie, Meg, and I talked about it and shared our grief. Marie was not as upset as I was, but I think she understood. Meg cried but got over it quickly. I suspect that while she regarded Anna as a playmate, it felt more like losing a cell phone app than a flesh-and-blood friend.

After Anna died—and that was how I thought of it—I threw myself into my work at Malloy with renewed vigor. In one sense, it was a way to honor Anna and the importance to her of meaningful values. That's what I told myself. But deeper down, it was probably a way to spackle over my grief and avoid admitting that she was gone. At some level, I felt that she might still be out there somewhere. That nagging hope helped me to understand better our human desire for certainty: I would rather know the truth, even if it were bad news, than continue to have to deal with the uncertainty. It was a conflict that could be truly resolved only through closure.

···········

The Project Manifesto implementation still wasn't easy. By the time Rita and I had worked with half the project teams to get their projects scheduled, we found that people were having trouble sticking to their project priorities—even though we had scheduled the highest priority projects first. Too many things seemed too critical; priorities were changing too often. Decisions seemed more and more difficult and people felt overloaded like never before. Some found themselves going back to the old way, setting priorities with deadlines and valuing responsiveness over whatever priorities they had. I began to fear we would have a rebellion.

I won't go into all the twists and turns Rita and I followed as we sought an answer. I sometimes felt like a rat trapped in a maze, not knowing whether we'd find cheese or a cat. I really missed Anna's ability to ask those obvious, annoying questions that provoked us to look at problems differently.

After talking with lots of people, we were able to distill our results into two types of comments. One was something like, "We're really short of resources, and we can't hire people because budgets are really tight." It was true: while there hadn't been any layoffs so far, there had also been very few new hires. The other type of comment was, "We're losing our position in the marketplace. We need more new products."

Due to these pressures, the Management Portfolio Team pushed more and more projects into R&D, with no changes to the work force, and expected to see progress. They seemed to believe that the more projects you start, the more you will finish. Rita and I started calling it the "spiritual" method for gating projects: if there was a prayer that someone could work on a project, they would create a project team and get it started. Maybe they thought that FD would be happy because everyone was going crazy. As a result, the work mounted, people jumped from task to task and project to project, and the pressure built.

When we sat down to analyze our findings, Rita's first comment was, "We're not following our values."

I gave the obvious answer. "You mean finishing over starting? Because it's obvious that just shoving more projects into the pipeline is only going to make things worse. Plumbing 101. Starting more projects won't help us finish more."

"We do need to value finishing over starting. We need to plan out how to implement our critical chain tools for managing the pipeline, so we start only those projects that we know can be finished without multitasking. But that's not the only problem. Rather than valuing priorities, everyone is trying to be responsive and make progress on all those new projects. They're losing sight of their priorities. It's a giant game of whack-a-mole."

"Most of the Management Portfolio Team is on our Senior Leadership Team. I think we need to have another discussion with them about the values, and decide how we're going to control project starts."

"I agree. But . . ." Rita looked into space for a moment, gathering her thoughts, then looked back at me and said, "We have problems with the first two values. We're starting stuff without finishing it; we're being responsive without clear priorities. I think we're not following through on the third value, either."

"What do you mean?"

"We're not valuing speed over deadlines. We have all these dates management says they 'need' the products to be ready on. They give them to customers, they give them to investors, they give them to project teams. People give those 'need' dates a huge amount of weight, but really they're deadlines. That's been bugging me a lot."

I wasn't convinced. "We can't get rid of management need dates. They're an important part of approving projects and communicating with customers. You can't judge whether to develop a product with no idea when it will be available. Need dates aren't the problem; people just have to value speed more."

"I think you're wrong. Those dates aren't based on reality. They're created before any real scheduling is done. They're based on guesses. And they're guesses with a predictable bias: if the dates are super-aggressive, we can squeeze people and make sure nobody is slacking off."

I laughed. "I hadn't really thought it through. I guess you're right. Ironic, that in trying to get people to work quickly, we create deadlines, which have exactly the opposite effect."

She leaned towards me as she stressed the importance of her point. "Sometimes the dates are improbable or impossible, and we still hold people to them. They really are deadlines. They dominate everyone's thinking. And they're killing our speed."

I sighed. "Probably so. People definitely spend a lot of time tweaking their schedules, trying to hit the need dates. I had thought it wasn't so important, because if people were working to speed—whatever date the schedule says—it'd still be as fast as possible." I thought a bit more and said, "I expect all that time people spend tweaking schedules only serves to make the schedules more and more biased, which means less and less realistic."

Rita smiled. "Which means, not only are need dates killing our speed, but they're also killing our ability to deliver on time."

We decided that pipeline management needed to be an urgent topic of our second Senior Leadership Team meeting. We wanted to look at all our projects as a single pipeline through which the work flowed, from ideas to products. We needed to agree on mechanisms for starting projects, assigning resources to them, and committing to "need" dates, in order to get products through the pipeline and onto the market as quickly as possible.

We had a great start: with our critical chain schedules, we were able to analyze resource loads, at least for a few key resources. It was credible data, in use by project teams, rather than made-up numbers reflecting arbitrary guesses. We could use the resource load information to reallocate people to where they were most needed and to make sure that people didn't start too many new projects.

We also brought the Senior Leadership and Management Portfolio Teams an approach for determining project "need" dates. We wanted to base the dates on real requirements, which meant doing some high-level scheduling while a project was still just an idea, before it was even given to a team. We would create "good enough" templates and plug them into the pipeline model to make sure we had sufficient resources to get the work done—at least approximately—without multitasking. When work began on a project, the team would create a more detailed schedule, using the template as a starting point. That might still cause the "need" date to be adjusted, but hopefully not by much.

....

Through the summer and fall, Rita and I kept the Project Manifesto moving ahead and it touched more and more areas. For example, our software people used "agile" techniques to develop software. While agile methodologies and the Agile Manifesto aren't in conflict with the Project Manifesto, some work is required to make sure the schedules line up. We worked with the software people to integrate their approach with our critical chain schedules.

We worked with the Six Sigma group to improve our project processes and develop a certification program. We planned that by the following summer, every manager would have at least a "green belt" certification in Project Manifesto concepts, tools, and techniques.

We kept up our communication plan and the regular flow of information. Rita and I sent reports to the

Senior Leadership Team, worked with project managers, and followed up with project teams. We organized meetings, interviews, surveys, and classes. Our measurement tools showed, for everyone to see, how the relay races were running and their impact on the whole organization. This transparency turned out to be key: while we like to believe that everyone wants to do the right thing, we know it's somehow more likely to happen when others are watching. In short, we did our best to follow our tenth work standard and communicate. I learned that when the communication starts to seem like too much, it's probably just about enough.

By the fall, pipeline management was up and running and an integral part of Malloy's process for managing its portfolio of projects. Projects had to be prioritized, and they weren't allowed to start until the Management Portfolio Team and the software said it was okay. Need dates were starting to make sense. Deadline measurements were gone. We had cemented the Project Manifesto values into the organization.

....

I remember exactly when I knew for sure that Rita would be a great person to lead the PMO forward. Our number-one project, code-named "Janus," was a little like Aurora—it had been limping along for several years, always predicted to be finished "soon" but never quite done. It was the first project we scheduled after the Project Manifesto rollout had begun. The schedule had shown five months of work left with about three months of buffer, taking us well into the next year. It wasn't what management wanted, but everyone had agreed that the schedule seemed credible.

As the Janus team learned to run the relay race, they didn't consume their buffer. In fact, they finished the project in early November with more buffer than they had in July. The gas gauge stayed full and the speed chart showed a wobbly line across its top. Rita and I met to do a postmortem in order to learn what we could from the experience.

I admitted that I was kind of disappointed. I said, "They must have been sandbagging."

"What do you mean?"

"They didn't use any buffer; in fact, they ended with more than a hundred percent of the buffer left. That means they must have been holding back on their focus durations."

"So what?"

"It means they were keeping safety time in the schedule. If we let that happen, we lose what we've been trying to do. When they made that schedule, they weren't following our fourth value, to value shared goals over individual goals."

Rita shook her head. "I think you've spotted a couple of trees and forgotten about the forest. They did have some extra time in the schedule, right?"

"Exactly."

"They didn't use that time up. Instead, they ran the relay race. Right?"

"Well, I guess so."

"In fact, they finished more than three months earlier than we thought. That's great, right?"

"Sure, but that doesn't get around the fact that their original schedule had extra time."

"Maybe so. But their behavior was exactly what we want, right?"

"Okay, but that's not my point. They should have done a better job with their schedule. Given the emphasis we're putting on recovering buffer, they stood to look a lot better if they created a bad schedule."

"Maybe, but first of all . . ." she started ticking off on her fingers, "nobody spotted it, and we have reviews for that kind of thing. Second, given how long this project has been going, it's not surprising that everyone wanted to be conservative. And third, they did a great job getting Janus done, so I think the team needs to be praised for their accomplishment. We need to understand if the schedule could have been better, but it would be a terrible idea to criticize great execution." Rita raised her eyebrows and gave me a quizzical look. "Right?"

She was irritatingly right. I felt stupid. "You're right." I thought back to Anna's final value, shaping the future over understanding the past. "Sounds like our most important job here is to figure out what went right and duplicate it."

Rita smiled. "Yep."

· · · · · · · · · · · ·

At home, Marie and I talked more and more about how we could integrate the things we loved with those we needed. We weren't indulging in wide-eyed dreams; we were actually thinking through those things we needed and those we loved, what made sense for us as a family and as individuals. Marie, Meg, and I were all making more deliberate choices in when and how we worked and in having positive interactions as a family. We planned events—weekends, movies, even trips to the ice cream parlor—to be fulfilling for all of us. We talked about what we were thinking and feeling. I didn't notice at the time how much those discussions were changing my life.

Marie seemed more supportive than ever as we got the PMO going. That may have been due more to changes in me than in her; maybe I was learning to accept

her support. Certainly I was relying more on her thinking. I know that she recognized and accepted the challenges I struggled with personally and professionally. As
time went by, we kept talking about our loves and needs
and got better at valuing what we loved. Despite all the
work in front of me, I found that our family was actually
becoming closer. There are many possible reasons, but I
like to think it's because of the values I followed at work
and at home.

············

Late in the summer, FD completed its acquisition of
Malloy. I received a tidy bonus for my work on Aurora.
It wasn't huge because I hadn't been on the project very
long and, with Aurora completed, was no longer considered indispensable. The other team members, Bert especially, were on track for much bigger payouts, but in order
to keep them around, FD spread their payments over several years.

That fall, the government's Department of Homeland
Security formed a joint task force with the Department of
Defense to research the impact of ANN technology on
cyber-terrorism. I suspect it was triggered by the earlier
virus threats exposed by Anna. The task force had several
careful discussions with FD's legal counsel. After assurances of confidentiality for FD's intellectual property, as

well as amnesty in case they might decide that FD or its employees had unwittingly done something wrong, we were all instructed to help. They started interviewing people at Malloy.

I was interviewed by two very serious, clean-cut men in their mid-thirties. They worked from a script and recorded everything. It took a couple of hours, starting with "what is your name?" and "how long have you been at Malloy Enterprises?" and eventually working around to Anna, ANN technology, and who might have had access to them. I didn't talk about Anna's being part of my family, because I felt that that was personal information and none of their business. But in other respects I didn't hold back. I'm not sure they fully believed everything I told them, but to their credit they remained professional and polite. As it happened, they had already talked with Bert and Andy, so I doubt there were any big surprises.

For my part, I wanted the government to understand that Anna was not the threat. To me, given her values and sacrifice, that seems beyond debate. Above all, I wanted them all to understand the importance of values. Single-minded focus on a goal can lead to ruin as everything else falls by the wayside. Without values, without thinking through and incorporating the reasons for our actions and the ways we resolve our conflicts, the ANN technology would present an unimaginable risk.

• • • • • • • • • • • •

At the start of our Project Manifesto rollout, many people at Malloy had real, understandable fears about making the switch to the relay race. They were worried about being unresponsive, but we weren't trying to create an unresponsive organization. We just needed to learn when it's important to be responsive. They were worried about minimizing deadlines, but we weren't trying to eliminate dates. We just needed to learn that faster is better.

By late December, we had demonstrated beyond any doubt the value of the Project Manifesto to Malloy and to FD. Malloy showed every sign of becoming one of FD's most successful businesses. We had gotten a couple of our highest-priority products developed and on the market. Our schedules showed us on track for 30 percent improvements in project durations or "cycle times," and based on data so far, we expected to meet our product launch windows at least 90 percent of the time. Productivity was hard to measure, but everyone claimed they were much more effective. Some of the benefits came from better planning and decision making. But I'm convinced that the majority came from our newfound ability to do focused work. The values helped us to focus on getting the important things done quickly, rather than over-valuing responsiveness and deadlines.

For the first time in three years, we had an end-of-year bonus pool at Malloy. It wasn't big, but it meant that even

FD recognized that we were on the right track. The relay race is now THE way projects are managed at Malloy. Senior management looks at speed charts all the time. Even Brian became a big believer. That shouldn't be too surprising, since as a result of our successes, "interim" was taken out of his job title and he became the permanent CEO of Malloy. What was more surprising was that I was beginning to think that I might learn to like the guy.

EPILOGUE

A s the new year began, I started to get restless. It's a big world out there with many interesting challenges and opportunities. With my management experience, I probably could have gotten a job with a different company fairly easily, but for me corporate America had lost its aura of inevitability. My discussions with Marie, as well as earlier discussions with Anna, had me thinking much more about what I wanted. And I wanted to see if there were people who would pay to implement the project values we had discovered: values that could dramatically improve speed, quality of life, and on-time performance. I had savings, a little year-end bonus money, and even some FD stock I could cash in. So early in the year, after much head scratching and agonizing and many family discussions, I decided to leave Malloy and go into business for myself. Marie and I were taking a risk, of course, but it looked like the logical next step in my journey to develop my Personal Manifesto.

There was no problem with my leaving Malloy. Rita could have started up the PMO without me, and with Brian's support I knew they would continue to improve on the work we had begun. I've kept in touch with the old Aurora team, and Rita and I continue to share what we learn. There's always something interesting going on.

So far, my consulting company has been very successful. Our first client was FD and its new meProducts division. Some of the people we worked with are old FD employees who were soured by years of corporate dysfunction and failed initiatives. FD has hired a lot of new kids as well, one of whom took over Aidan's position as GM. I've found that if we communicate enough about the right things, even the most cynical people eventually hop on board with both feet. The Project Manifesto makes sense, and people want to do things that make sense.

I love my work, but I do miss Anna. With the threat she represented dealt with, I think the government is more likely to focus on using the ANN technology rather than stifling it. But they don't share their views with me, and there's no telling what the future holds. Will they try to create another Anna, in order to use her to protect us from threats? If history is any judge, they're more likely to try to create a weapon. What are the risks? What are the costs? What values will they instill in their creations?

A few days ago, I received a small package in the mail with no return address. It contained only a high-capacity computer thumb drive. It could be nothing. It could be from Anna. She did promise she would try to save herself. It could also be from someone or something else, maybe someone who wants to find out what I know about the ANN technology. Frankly, the thumb drive terrifies me. But I expect I'll have to decide soon what to do with it. Right now, it looks pretty clear what that decision will have to be. After all, I am still looking for closure.

PROJECT MANIFESTO VALUES, STANDARDS, AND SCHEDULING

This Addendum consolidates the final form of the different lists that appear throughout the text. If you are interested in a more comprehensive explanation of these concepts, you can download the free Project Manifesto Field Guide. Sign up at *http://www.prochain.com/projectmanifesto* for the Field Guide and other related resources.

The Project Manifesto Values

The Project Manifesto values describe conflicts that people frequently feel when doing project work. The values give a direction for resolving the conflicts: We value A over B. B is important, but it should be put in the context of A.

Paradigm: Relay Race

1. We value priorities over responsiveness.
2. We value finishing over starting.

---

3. We value speed over deadlines.
4. We value shared goals over individual goals.

Work Standards

The work standards are concrete, actionable ways of expressing the Project Manifesto. They provide a shared way of looking at the values.

Standard #1: Work to your priorities.

Standard #2: Agree on global priorities, taking into account relative value.

Standard #3: Work tasks from start to finish, as quickly as possible; then hand off the work.

Standard #4: Create credible project schedules that include the work of all functions.

Standard #5: Each day, determine your top-priority task.

Standard #6: Report honest status (days remaining) to the best of your ability.

Standard #7: Look for ways to improve focus. When working on key tasks, minimize meetings; turn off email, instant messaging, and phones; find quiet places to work.

Standard #8: Don't switch to lower-priority tasks; avoid asking and avoid agreeing.

Standard #9: Work as a team to share and recover buffer time.

Standard #10: When in doubt, communicate. Both ways.

The Update Checklist

Use of checklists is an excellent way to ensure that simple procedures are followed and important things get done. This update checklist is one example. If you have weekly project team meetings, it can serve as an agenda to ensure that people are thinking about the important things.

- ☐ Make sure all updates are entered into the schedule.
- ☐ Make sure everyone is present.
- ☐ Discuss any needed changes to the schedule.
- ☐ Review project issues and risks.
- ☐ Discuss what's key (on or near the critical chain).
- ☐ Talk about how we can help each other recover buffer.
- ☐ Determine whether anything is blocked and, if so, fix it.
- ☐ Share better ways of running the relay race.

Roger's Scheduling Process and Rules

Roger's view of a scheduling process is certainly simple. It is not a detailed primer on how to schedule a project. But we do believe that Roger's scheduling process and rules are a great place to start to create better schedules and improve your project management.

1. Start with a project charter.
2. Create a high-level map of the needed work.
3. Build your project schedule by starting at the end of the project and working earlier in time.
4. Keep the schedule current.

And here are Roger's scheduling rules:

- Maximize credibility—for everyone.
- Create and maintain the schedule with the whole team.
- Have as few endpoints as possible.
- Make sure all task names, except possibly a few key milestones, have verbs and objects.
- Understand "done" for every task.
- Use focus durations and protect the schedule with buffers.

The Personal Manifesto

>   Roger's value: I value what I love over what I need.
>   Anna's value: I value shaping the future over
>   understanding the past.

These "Personal Manifesto" values are ideas that we have found to be helpful. You may or may not agree with them; you may come up with your own. When a certain type of situation repeatedly presents you with difficult conflicts, it can help to use the Manifesto approach. Identify the conflict; think about what you value; see if one side can be put in the context of the other; and work through some examples. At the very least, the process should give you a different slant on problems and reveal new ways to approach them.

As an exercise, consider under what circumstances you might value others' opinions or authority over your own. Can you express your conclusions as a value?

APPLYING THE
PROJECT MANIFESTO

During his senior year in high school, Rob started a bicycle club. To do that, he put an ad in the school bulletin that read: "The first meeting of the bicycle club will take place on the library steps at 3 P.M. on Thursday." Only a couple of other kids showed up, so they all went home, agreeing that the bicycle club was an idea the world wasn't ready for. Imagine Rob's surprise, reading the next bulletin, to discover an ad for the next bicycle club meeting. It turns out that the library had sets of stairs on opposite sides of the building. Rob and a few others logically waited on the side with the most steps. The cool kids waited on the side where the cool kids hung out. They started up the club without him. Being ashamed, and initially pretty confused, Rob never went to a meeting.

This story is about miscommunication, but it's also about habits and assumptions. The cool kids were in the habit of meeting on the library steps, so they "knew" where to go. Rob and a few others did not share that habit, so they made an assumption. No one bothered to check their assumptions, because *no one even recognized that they had made an assumption.*

Most of our decisions are instinctive, based on assumptions and habits that we don't think about and often don't even recognize. That's not unreasonable, because we can't possibly think through every decision. Psychologist Daniel Kahneman talks about two systems people use to make decisions: System 1, which is quick and imprecise and doesn't require a lot of energy; and System 2, which is slow, deliberate, and inefficient. We don't have the time or energy to make all our decisions with System 2. The good news: We have great mechanisms for developing shortcuts. We adopt values. We create habits. The bad news: Where the habits start, the thinking stops. When the environment changes, the habits don't.

We urgently need to think more about personal productivity. We need new habits and new assumptions. Despite the chronic lack of time we all experience and complain about, we continue to waste our time.

The traditional values on which the Project Manifesto is based all have logical roots. For example, when a person starts a new job, she might say, "I've got to keep this job. I have to please my boss and my more experienced colleagues." She develops a System 1 routine that says "Be responsive." She makes a habit of being responsive by working hard to keep everyone happy. She picks up the phone during dinner, interrupts a critical document review to dispense advice, or works late hours because there's stuff to do. She multitasks all the time. That responsiveness often keeps her from doing the things that are truly important; whether that's eating dinner, reviewing the document, or spending time with her family. It also burgeons into a measurement system: responsiveness should be rewarded.

The other traditional values are similar. We get started on new things that pop into our brains or in-boxes. We try to hit every deadline. We try to meet our individual goals. As we discussed in the book, all of these traditional values frequently cause us to be less productive and more stressed.

The difficulties we have in changing habits leads to an important question: How can you adopt the Project Manifesto values? There's a set of obvious answers:

- Use tools, like critical chain scheduling, that help you to set clear, stable priorities for project tasks.
- Use the PICK ME approach to help prioritize all your work.
- Carve out time for focused work and guard it jealously.

- Don't start working on something new if
  you've already started something at least as
  important that you should be finishing.
- Every time you see a due date, evaluate it. Would
  earlier be better? Is late necessarily a disaster?
- Think about the individual goals you work
  towards. Does each goal really matter? Does
  it get in the way of more important goals?
- Get the people around you on board with the
  Project Manifesto.

These are good answers. Unfortunately, they aren't things we're used to doing. They come face to face with our ingrained habits. That means that despite a lot of work and thought, we're likely to have trouble changing.

To find a better answer, let's consider the structure of habits. According to Charles Duhigg, a New York Times reporter who has written and lectured extensively on the subject, at the core of a habit is a neurological loop that consists of three parts: cue, routine, and reward. The cue triggers the habit. The routine is the habitual behavior that is triggered. And the reward is something desirable that causes you to repeat the habit. For example, consider habitual gambling. Different people may have different cues that provoke them to gamble, such as money in the pocket, a difficult time at home, or even the act of driving by a casino. Once the behavior is cued, you experience a craving for the reward, so you perform the routine. You gamble. The "reward" that reinforces the gambling behavior might be an escape from day-to-day worries or the release of dopamine into the brain.

It isn't easy to break habits. We usually attack them by trying to stop the behavior. If you examine the list of "obvious" answers above, you'll see that they all directly attack traditional behaviors. Unfortunately, when the cues and rewards remain in place, behaviors are very difficult to change directly. Duhigg points out that you can be much more effective in changing habits by addressing the cue or the reward. Without the cue, the behavior isn't triggered. Without the reward, we don't experience the craving.

You can think of the traditional values in the Project Manifesto as habits. The "be responsive" habit might be triggered by someone walking by your cubicle, the phone ringing, or an email icon appearing on your computer. Table 1 shows some different cues, routines, and rewards associated with the traditional values.

Traditional value	Cued by . . .	Triggers a routine . . .	Resulting in rewards . . .
Be responsive	Interruptions (phone ringing, an email icon appearing, someone passing by your cubicle); the mental churn of having many things to do	Stop what you're doing and work on something else	Appreciation from others; a feeling that you've done the right thing
Get things started	Something new in the inbox; a new idea	Start something new rather than finishing something that you've already started	Appreciation from others; a feeling that you've done the right thing; the excitement of tackling something new
Work to deadlines	A date for something to be completed	Adjust work execution to meet those dates	Appreciation from others; a feeling that you've done the right thing; individual or team incentives
Meet individual goals	Individual performance goals set by or with management	Adjust work to meet those goals	Organizational status and/or incentives

Table 1: Traditional Values as Habits

The work standards discussed in this book can help you to attack many of these cues and rewards, especially if you and your co-workers understand and agree to the standards. For example, Standard 7 provides a framework to avoid cues that trigger undesired behaviors: "Look for ways to improve focus. When working on key tasks, minimize meetings; turn off email, instant messaging, and phones; find quiet places to work."

All these ideas might not be enough. It's hard for any one of us to have the discipline to follow the Project Manifesto. Changing work behaviors across an organization is much harder; it requires synchronized commitment and self-discipline from many people. Here's another idea that might help eliminate cues that trigger undesired behaviors: hire mentors to stand at everyone's shoulder, pointing out each time they're about to screw up. We might hire spouses to provide that service, in much the same way they help to improve our driving.

The "mentor" idea isn't really feasible, and if it were, you'd soon have to do your mentor grievous bodily harm. But it does suggest another answer: daily reminders. Become more mindful of your values through daily reminders that reinforce those values. This idea is incorporated into Standard 5: "Each day, determine your top-priority task." If you follow Standard 5, you will at least spend a little time every day thinking about your work in a holistic way.

There is an even better reminder system: daily emails that appear in your inbox each morning to remind you to think about how well you are following the Project Manifesto values. If you sign up at *http://www.prochain.com/ dailyquestions*, each morning you will be sent an email that asks a set of questions like the following (answer each question using a scale of 0-6):

- How clear and specific are your top priorities for today?
- How well did you **work to your priorities** yesterday?
- How well did you focus on your work and minimize interruptions yesterday?
- How well did you communicate with your colleagues yesterday?
- How well were you able to finish old work before starting new work yesterday?
- Yesterday, how well did you resist changing your priorities in order to hit lower-priority deadlines?
- To what extent do you think your priorities are aligned with the top priorities for the organization?

After signing up, you will get this email every work day for four weeks. You can respond at any time, although we recommend doing it in the morning when you carry out Standard 5 ("Each day, determine your top-priority task"). You can log in to see how your numbers have changed over time.

Of course, you can opt out of this email at any time. Your name and email address are safe: ProChain will not use your information except to provide you with data, and for aggregate research purposes in which no one is identified. We also recommend that you log in and poke around from time to time, as we plan to continue adding functionality.

NOTES

Acknowledgements

viii **Dr. Eliyahu M. Goldratt, whose groundbreaking work challenging people's assumptions and provoking their intuition** Dr. Goldratt died in 2011, but he left a brilliant legacy. His most famous and influential book is E. Goldratt (2012), *The Goal: A Process of Ongoing Improvement, 3rd ed.* (Great Barrington, MA: North River Press). He also wrote the first book describing critical chain scheduling: E. Goldratt (1997), *Critical Chain* (Great Barrington, MA: North River Press).

Chapter 1: Anna

3 **the lady who did all the voice messages for the phone company.** Yes, there was such a lady; see, for example, "Jane Barbe" (2013) in *Wikipedia, the free encyclopedia*, retrieved from *http://en.wikipedia.org/wiki/Jane_Barbe*.

Chapter 2: Values

25   project charter document   Formally, a project charter is "A document initiated by the project initiator or sponsor that formally authorizes the existence of a project and provides the project manager with the authority to apply organizational resources to project activities." Project Management Institute (2013), *A guide to the project management body of knowledge (PMBOK® Guide)*, *5th ed.* (Newtown Square, PA: Project Management Institute), 553.

29   one of the job requirements   You can find many jobs that ask for multitasking skills on *http://www.monster .com*, especially under management categories like "Project/Program Management."

29   I read an article about multitasking recently. There are many references discussing the impact of multitasking on quality and productivity. The story of Andrew Heit's death while texting gained national attention; see *http://www.greeleytribune.com/news/6070548-113/driving-text-texting-heit*. One researcher found that information workers were interrupted on average every three minutes. V. Gonzalez and G. Mark (2004), "Constant, Constant, Multi-tasking Craziness: Managing Multiple Working Spheres," *Proceedings of ACM CHI'04*, 116. Researchers also found that the average length of time that information workers spent before being interrupted was 11 minutes. G. Mark, V. Gonzalez and J. Harris (2005), "No Task Left Behind? Examining the Nature of Fragmented Work," *Proceedings of ACM CHI'04*, 324.

31 Task A takes seven days to finish, except it's probably a lot more Andy's major point in the story is the impact of multitasking on task and project durations. This topic is rarely discussed; see R. Newbold (2008), *The Billion Dollar Solution: Secrets of ProChain Project Management* (Lake Ridge, VA: ProChain Press), 43–47. The Web page *http://www.prochain.com/games/multitasking.html* gives a useful hands-on demonstration of the productivity and cycle time problems associated with multitasking.

33 A relay race is exactly what we should be running. The relay race is sometimes called the "roadrunner" work ethic: when there is work to do, work it at full speed to completion and then pass it on; otherwise, do nothing. J. Cox, L. Boyd, T. Sullivan, R. Reid, and B. Cartier (2012), *The Theory of Constraints International Certification Organization Dictionary, Second Edition* (Washington: Theory of Constraints International Certification Organization), 108. The term "roadrunner" is more common in the manufacturing world.

36 This reminds me of the Agile Manifesto. For a more complete story, check *http://agilemanifesto.org*.

Chapter 3: Risks

46   You may have heard of the Eliza program   See "Eliza" (2013) in *Wikipedia, the free encyclopedia*, retrieved from *http://en.wikipedia.org/wiki/ELIZA*. As of this writing, you can talk with Eliza at *http://www.masswerk.at/elizabot/*.

Chapter 4: Scheduling

54   One of the biggest causes of project failure is inadequate planning.   Inadequate planning consistently falls near or at the top of the list in surveys regarding the causes of project failure, but better planning does take more time. "[The most successful project managers] allocated just over twice as much time toward project planning as their counterparts." A. Crowe (2006), *Alpha Project Managers: What the Top 2% Know that Everyone Else Does Not* (Kennesaw, GA: Velociteach), 107.

60   everything will take longer.   See, for example, *http://www.prochain.com/games/projstarts.html* for a simple but instructive exercise.

60   we start things without noticing, without saying, "now that we've started this, what else are we NOT going to work on?"   That happens frequently with improvement projects. It's common for organizations to have dozens of improvement projects "in process," with no clear priorities to distinguish them. It's not surprising that multitasking is rampant and that improvement projects are very difficult to complete.

62 This shows the critical chain, the set of tasks that really determines the completion date. "The [critical chain is the] longest sequence of dependent events through a project network considering both task and resource dependencies in completing the project. The critical chain is the constraint of a project." J. Cox et al, *The Theory of Constraints International Certification Organization Dictionary*, 35.

67 Standard #5: Each day, determine your top-priority task. The rationale behind this standard is discussed further in Appendix B. Its purpose is to create greater awareness of one's correct priorities.

68 Regular meetings are a good way to monitor the schedule and risk. At ProChain we typically recommend weekly meetings, but for critical and/or shorter-term projects, daily standups can be a good idea.

68 Making them into frequent standups can be a good way to build teamwork. This is a standard technique and a formal part of the agile "Scrum" approach; see, e.g.,

"Scrum (software development)" (2013) in *Wikipedia, the free encyclopedia*, retrieved from *http://en.wikipedia.org/wiki/Scrum_(development)*.

68   I hate percent complete, because I never know what it means.   Reporting "percent complete" is common, especially with those using Earned Value Management, but—"If you want real status, collect instead the duration remaining; it is far clearer. If a four-day task was 25 percent complete on Tuesday and 40 percent complete on Thursday, when will it finish?" Newbold, *The Billion Dollar Solution*, 160.

Chapter 5: Deadlines

75   I didn't know they were going to be off track. Two related syndromes are relevant here. One, Bert's problem, occurs when someone is behind but doesn't want to report bad news because they hope they can get back on track. Another, known as "schedule chicken," occurs when people don't admit to problems because they hope someone else will have to admit to a delay first and thereby take the blame. In either case, by the time the delays are reported, there is much less opportunity to address them. Too often we see projects that seem to be going really well, until the last minute, when suddenly they're not.

78 The deadlines have to slow down the race. And this is the problem, as discussed in detail in R. Newbold (2013), "The Tyranny of Deadlines," originally published in the proceedings of the 2013 PMI Scheduling Community of Practice Conference and also available at *http://www. prochain.com/pm/articles/Tyranny_of_Deadlines.pdf.* Deadlines are a common and unchallenged paradigm. Consider this quote: "Project assignments always have deadlines. So even though you're not sure what your new project is to accomplish, you want to know when it has to be finished." S. Portny (2013), *Project Management for Dummies*, 4ᵗʰ ed. (Hoboken, NJ: John Wiley & Sons), 107. A famous quote attributed to Napoleon Hill says, "A goal is a dream with a deadline." The implication isn't just that people can't accomplish anything without a deadline; it's that they shouldn't even try.

80 Sometimes I do have to give students deadlines to get them to do anything. For a real-life demonstration that students can perform better when there are deadlines, see D. Ariely (2010), *Predictably Irrational, Revised and Expanded Edition* (New York: Harper Collins), 142–145. It seems clear that if someone really doesn't want to do something, they will tend to procrastinate.

85 It figured that scheduling would be the easy part. It is common for people to become far too fixated on technology as separate from methodology, and the tail ends up wagging the dog. For example, people typically place great emphasis on scheduling tools and technologies and almost none on the behaviors those technologies will need to support. It is essential to understand how new tools are going to be used to create benefits, before committing to their deployment. We have seen companies spend millions of dollars on systems that, in the end, gave them little or no value.

86   some software provides a new alternative to feeding buffers.   *The newer approach appears to me to be simple and logical.* ProChain software supports feeding buffers, but our preferred approach is to calculate the needed protection time, and either use it to move feeding chains earlier and protect the critical chain (if there is available time or "slack") or put it into the project buffer. Rather than tracking feeding buffer consumption, we calculate the likely effect of these integration points and look at changes over time.

Chapter 6: Buffers

93   you can take into account the possibility of delays where non-critical work integrates with the critical chain.   If several inputs are needed in order to start work on a particular task, a delay on any of the inputs will delay work on the task. That means tasks that have multiple inputs are often at higher risk for delays. This effect is called "merge bias" or "integration risk."

93   You can also consider cases where critical chain task durations are very likely or unlikely to be hit.   The range of possible durations for a critical chain task may be very wide or very narrow, in which case the contribution of such a task to the buffer may be very large or very small. For example, heat testing a product may require that it sit in an oven for exactly two weeks, in which case that task should contribute nothing to the buffer. On the other hand, if you have to invent a new technology or wait for a congressional budget to pass, there may never be enough buffer.

93   Sometimes Monte Carlo simulation is used. There is also the "sum of squares" approach, described in R. Newbold (1998), *Project Management in the Fast Lane: Applying the Theory of Constraints* (Boca Raton: St. Lucie Press), 94. We don't recommend either approach, because both approaches generally assume that project tasks are *independent* and that delays in one place are likely to be canceled by speedups elsewhere. But if the tasks are not independent, which is almost always true in the project world, a delay in one place may imply delays in other places. As a result, Monte Carlo techniques will often create buffers that are too small to accommodate real variation.

Chapter 7: Focus

101 I've always found that if you give people aggressive targets, and measure them against those targets, they'll perform better. This is a common belief. For example, "Commitment to deadlines helps employees focus their efforts on completing the goal on or before the due date." R. Nelson (2010), *Managing for Dummies* (Hoboken, NJ: Wiley Publishing), 106. Sometimes people do perform better with aggressive targets in front of them, but be sure they are motivated to *beat* target dates, not just meet them.

104 Sometimes he ended up working from home or holing up with me in 6F to avoid interruptions. When people absolutely have to get something done, they change the way they work in order to be able to focus. Focusing means more productivity and more speed.

Chapter 9: Understanding

123 We turned my informal agenda for standup meetings into a more formal Update Checklist: Checklists are a great way to create flexible processes and still make sure certain things are accomplished. They are common in aviation. More recently, they've been used in hospital operating rooms to dramatically decrease the incidence of nosocomial infections. For an excellent discussion, see A. Gawande (2009), *The Checklist Manifesto: How to Get Things Right* (New York: Metropolitan Books).

127   After all, deadlines get people moving. Maybe the stress did help me to go faster. This effect is certainly a major justification for deadlines. And in fact, "Short-term stressors of mild to moderate severity enhance cognition, while major or prolonged stressors are disruptive." R. Sapolsky (2004), *Why Zebras Don't Get Ulcers, 3rd ed.* (New York: St. Martin's Griffin), 204. The real problem is with prolonged stress, as Sapolsky discusses in detail.

128   I wondered about the impact of stress on creativity and productivity. Later, I did some research and discovered that the impact over time can be big. It's not hard to find references. Performance under stress can vary significantly depending on the individual and the type of work. Generally speaking, over the short term, performance follows a U-shaped curve (the "Yerkes-Dodson Law"): performance increases up to a certain level of stress and then decreases. Prolonged stress can cause numerous significant negative effects, as described in Sapolsky, *Why Zebras Don't Get Ulcers*. In many organizations, deadlines are used intentionally to create prolonged stress for employees. DeMarco talks persuasively about the need for less stress in order for people to be more productive in T. DeMarco (2001), *Slack: Getting Past Burnout, Busywork, and the Myth of Total Efficiency* (New York: Broadway Books).

Chapter 10: Disconnects

150   **then you have to reset the timer to thirty minutes.** This is borrowed from the Pomodoro Technique®, *http://www.pomodorotechnique.com/*, an approach to improving work and study habits.

Chapter 12: Transfer

171   **we've got our Six Sigma and lean programs**   Lean manufacturing is a management philosophy derived from the Toyota Manufacturing System. It is generally focused on reducing waste and improving the flow of work through an organization. Six Sigma is a set of tools and processes that are primarily centered on eliminating defects and reducing process variability. Lean manufacturing and Six Sigma tools are being applied more and more in Research and Development organizations. The tools can be useful in improving relay race processes.

173   So . . . marketing is a big part of implementing the Project Manifesto?   The ProChain philosophy of implementation management is described in R. Newbold, "Making Change Stick," which is Chapter 5 of J. Cox and J. Schleier, Jr. (2010), *Theory of Constraints Handbook* (New York: McGraw Hill) and is also published separately. We call the approach CoRe, which stands for Cycle of Results. It involves setting expectations, building ownership, creating value, and verifying the results.

173   that's a big reason why we see so many improvement initiatives come and go.   Everyone has stories about failed initiatives, but it's hard to find organizations willing to talk about them. See the discussion of the "Uptake Problem" in Newbold, "Making Change Stick," 102–103.

Chapter 13: Rollout

183   how do you measure people?   Communicate frequently about how people are doing. Can they focus? Is the quality of their work good? How does their speed compare with what we would expect from the position? Don't use arbitrary deadlines.

183   When is it okay to say "no" or "not now"?   As long as people understand and agree on the priorities, it

should be okay any time to postpone lower-priority work. Management can decide to override existing priorities if a particular task or project is important enough.

183   How should work be prioritized?   We recommend the PICK ME method, described in the text, as a guide for prioritizing individuals' work. To prioritize project work, we recommend that priorities be set according to how far tasks are from being key (i.e., how far from being on the critical chain) and according to project priorities. Discussions about priorities can get very involved because there are many variables. For example, we encounter two types of projects: projects that must be finished on a particular date (e.g., a stadium for a sporting event), and projects that should be finished as quickly as possible. If the relative value of projects varies significantly, you'll need to consider that as well. Should you work on a key task for project X, or an almost-key task for project Y? Often, you'll work the task for project X—unless project Y is much more valuable. In any case, if you know relative project importance and how far tasks are from being key, you're most of the way there. It's far better to pick priorities and work to them, than to multitask.

188   these kinds of incentive plans just aren't worth much.   Research shows that incentive plans rarely accomplish what they were intended to accomplish. For the classic, if somewhat lopsided, indictment of incentive plans, see A. Kohn (1993), *Punished by Rewards: The Trouble with Gold Stars, Incentive Plans, A's, Praise, and Other Bribes* (New York: Houghton Mifflin Harcourt).

192   measurements to see how people are doing with the values.   Feedback matters. For a current perspective, see D. Garvin, A. Wagonfeld, and L. Kind (2013), "Google's Project Oxygen: Do Managers Matter?" (Harvard Business School Publishing, Boston, MA).

Chapter 14: Reminders

197   starting things that could be finished   One important technique is called "full kitting," which means making sure that necessary approvals and materials are available before tasks or projects are started. J. Cox et al, *The Theory of Constraints International Certification Organization Dictionary*, 58.

198   routine habits were heavily ingrained   See Appendix B.

198   assessing how people were really performing wasn't easy.   At the individual level, evaluating performance based on meeting deadlines is at best one small measure of how good an employee is. It's more important to have open communication about people's productivity, the quality of their work, their attitude, and so on.

198 automated reminder system When you want to change behaviors, daily reminders can be valuable to keep the changes fresh in your mind. See, for example, M. Goldsmith (2006), "Questions That Make a Difference Every Day," accessed from *http://www.marshall goldsmithlibrary.com/docs/Talent-Management/Questions-Make-Difference-TM.doc*. Check Appendix B for more information on reminders.

Chapter 15: Expanding

210 start the projects that we know can be finished without multitasking. Excess work in process, meaning more projects than the organization can work without multitasking, can promote multitasking and slow everything down. It generates additional variation and quality problems and makes predictability even more difficult. You can find a great discussion of the evils of manufacturing work in process in E. Goldratt and R. Fox (1986), *The Race* (Croton-on-Hudson, New York: North River Press), 52–66. The concepts in that book map very well to the world of projects.

211   Sometimes the dates are improbable or impossible, and we still hold people to them.   This is the heart of the problem: people are forced to commit to dates that may not be realistic, creating all the problems of deadlines. In fact, the real situation is worse, because very often people will make the schedules unrealistic in order to match the dates. Not only do organizations need a rational process to determine need dates, but they also need a schedule review process that aligns expectations among management and workers. See Newbold, *The Billion Dollar Solution*, Appendix B: "Old Game/New Game."

212   reallocate people to where they were most needed, and to make sure that people didn't start too many new projects.   The basic question behind pipeline management is how to pace the start of projects in such a way that there's neither too little nor too much to work on. The typical management response is to start enough projects so that there's no question that there's too much work. Unfortunately, that approach also guarantees overloads and increases the chances of multitasking. There are a couple of Critical Chain approaches. One is to use a small number of pacing resources (ideally, one) and push out or pace some projects in order to minimize overloads on those pacing resources. For a more complete discussion, see Newbold, *The Billion Dollar Solution*, Chapter 16.

213 **While agile methodologies and the Agile Mani-festo are not in conflict with the Project Manifesto, some work is required to make sure the schedules line up.** This can be done by using agile "iterations" or "sprints" to manage the low-level work and using resource-loaded project schedules to manage higher-level work. See R. Newbold (2009), "Agile and Critical Chain," referenced at *http://www.prochain.com/prochain_blog/?cat=15*. For a view on critical chain scheduling that incorporates agile and other methodologies (including Theory of Constraints and Kanban), see S. Tendon and S. Müller (2013), *Tame the Flow: Hyper-Productive Knowledge Work Management.* (Leanpub: *https://leanpub.com/tame-the-flow*).

214 **we know it's somehow more likely to happen when others are watching.** This is a demonstrated phenomenon. What you might not know is that just an image of eyes can keep people more honest; see M. Bateson, D. Nettle, and G. Roberts (2006), "Cues of Being Watched Enhance Cooperation in Real-World Setting," *Biology Letters* 2, no. 3 (September), 412–414, referenced at *http://www.ncbi.nlm.nih.gov/pmc/articles/PMC1686213/*.

Epilogue

223 **improve speed, quality of life, and on-time performance.** This is the ultimate irony: if you value speed over deadlines, due-date performance is much better than if you value deadlines over speed.

Appendix B: Applying the Project Manifesto

234 Psychologist Daniel Kahneman talks about See D. Kahneman (2011), *Thinking, Fast and Slow* (New York: Farrar, Straus and Giroux) for an excellent and comprehensive discussion of this topic, with many references to the associated psychological experiments and literature.

236 According to Charles Duhigg Duhigg covers this material in detail in C. Duhigg (2013), *The Power of Habit: Why We Do What We Do in Life and Business* (New York: Random House). See especially Chapter 1, "The Habit Loop," and the appendix, "A Reader's Guide to Using These Ideas."

240 There is an even better reminder system This is the approach discussed in Goldsmith, "Questions That Make a Difference Every Day" (*http://www.marshallgold smithlibrary.com/docs/Talent-Management/Questions-Make-Difference-TM.doc*).